NORMAN ENGLAND

This survey follows naturally on Mr. Sellman's earlier Outlines of Prehistoric Britain, Roman Britain, The Anglo-Saxons and The Vikings. In a very real sense it is continuation of the last two, for it shows us what happened when the Norman descendants of the Vikings crossed the Channel to conquer and mingle with the Anglo-Saxons.

After dealing with the Conquest, Mr. Sellman surveys all the more important aspects of life in Norman England. He has illustrated the book with many maps and diagrams, while Kenneth Ody has contributed a number of drawings that bring the contemporary scene vividly to life.

Poaching the King's deer

METHUEN'S (M) OUTLINES

NORMAN ENGLAND

by

R. R. SELLMAN

Illustrated by the Author and

KENNETH ODY

METHUEN & CO LTD

36 ESSEX STREET . STRAND . LONDON W.C. 2

First published 1959
© 1959 R. R. Sellman
Printed and bound in Great Britain
by W. & J. Mackay & Co. Ltd., Chatham

CATALOGUE NO 6173/U

CONTENTS

Ploughing (*Bayeux Tapestry*)

THE Norman Conquest is by long tradition the most outstanding event in English history. We number our kings from it, ignoring the Saxon Edwards, and from some accounts one might imagine that it marked the beginning of English kingship and civilisation. It was hardly that, for England at the time was an older, richer, and in many ways more civilised country than Normandy, and the Crown of Alfred's successors was ancient and venerable compared with the coronet of the upstart Norman dukes.

ENGLAND AND NORMANDY

The hard-headed and hard-fisted Viking chiefs and warbands to whom the French king Charles the Simple had granted land in 911, as a barrier to further raiding up his northern rivers, had been less numerous than the Danes who settled the English Danelaw. They and their descendants had remained a ruling warrior class, keeping alive the Viking spirit by further aggressions against their neighbours. They were slow to accept Christianity, some remaining pagan to the end of the tenth century, and the feeble-ness of the French monarchs barred any attempt to assimilate them by force. They learnt readily enough from the French whatever was of immediate practical use, such as the crafts of fighting on horse-back and building in stone; but their ideas of law and government remained those of a warrior society.

Their dukes ruled practically as independent kings, though in name vassals of the King of France. Having no long tradition behind them, as English rulers had, their authority depended solely on their own strength and personality. There was nothing comparable to the ancient English shire system for justice and administration, and they had to evolve an arrangement which would give them an army and keep them supreme while relieving them of responsibility for minor business. Feudalism was not a Norman invention, but in Normandy it became much more tightly organised and effective than elsewhere. The Duchy was small enough for most of the greater lords to be relations of the Duke, and for the Duke's nearness to discourage any ideas of independence or rebellion. An

NORMANDY

DEPENDENCIES OF WILLIAM

IN 1066

NORTH-UMBRIA

York

Chester

Lincoln

ENGLAND

Shrewsbury

WALES

MERCIA

Hereford

Norwich

London

WESSEX

Winchester

Dover

Exeter

Hastings

FLANDERS (in temporary alliance with William)

St. Valery

Bayeux

Rouen

Caen

Coutances

NORMANDY

Mantes

Falaise

Paris

Domfront

Alençon

Dol

MAINE

BRITTANY

Rennes

Le Mans

Orleans

FRANCE

Angers

ANJOU

Nantes

Tours

0   50   100 M.

aristocratic warrior society, which had no need to rely on an armed free peasantry as in England, could adopt without difficulty the principle that all land was held directly or indirectly from the Duke on condition of mounted military service.

The Dukes were prime movers in establishing the Church in Normandy, and they kept it, like everything else, under their close control. They appointed bishops and abbots, treated Church lands almost as their own property, and even refused to allow any interference by the Pope without their sanction. At the same time, with the zeal of new converts, they co-operated willingly in the new movements for Church reform; and Normandy was certainly more closely affected by these than was relatively isolated England.

The Normans were not notably civilised, and in most of the arts of peace they could not compare with the English. Where they excelled was in capacity and readiness for aggressive war.

England showed striking contrasts. The prestige of the Crown was so great that Edward the Confessor—who could not have lasted six weeks as Duke of Normandy—died tranquilly in his palace after a reign of twenty-four years in which he proved himself more fitted for an abbey than a throne. The powers of an English king were such as Duke William might, and in fact did, envy; but Edward's feeble grasp of the reins had allowed over-mighty earls to reach a degree of independence which threatened to make the English monarchy as nominal as that of France.

England was far larger and more populous than Normandy, but it was not organised for aggressive war. The recent continental development of cavalry fighting, which had made the armoured knight master of the battlefield, had not crossed the Channel; and such haphazard beginnings of feudalism as had emerged from the Danish wars were a matter of personal ties between lord and man. Fighting strength lay firstly in the royal bodyguard of Housecarles (a legacy of Canute), secondly in the well-equipped thegns of the countryside, and finally in the fyrd of freemen. Housecarles and thegns had horses and were reasonably mobile, though the thegns might take long to muster; but the fyrd could only in practice be drawn from a few shires near the point of danger, and it could not feed itself (as an invader could) by ravaging the land without thought for the inhabitants. For purely defensive purposes, against Vikings who also fought on foot, this system could suffice under vigorous leadership: but beside the new feudal armies of the Continent it was out-of-date.

England had long been a target for Viking ambitions, and the last serious Scandinavian invasion was yet to come in 1066. In spirit the Normans were Vikings still, as their exploits in Sicily had recently shown, and in addition they were now much better armed and organised than their Scandinavian kinsmen had ever been. It is not surprising that they looked across the Channel to Edward's rich but militarily backward kingdom with sinister interest.

Ties between the English and Norman ruling families had existed for more than half a century. The unhappy Ethelred had married a Norman wife, Emma, and

3

had taken refuge in Normandy with his sons at the time of Sweyn's conquest in 1013. After Ethelred's death their mother married Canute, but the two princes remained in Normandy and were brought up as Normans. The elder died in 1036; and with the death of the last Danish king in 1042 Edward returned, when already in middle age, to claim the throne. Many Normans followed him, and were appointed to high places in Church and State, with the result that English resentment gathered under Earl Godwine of Wessex. After a brief exile in 1051, the Earl returned in force and obliged Edward to dismiss many of the foreigners. According to Norman sources it was during the Earl's absence that William of Normandy (Edward's second cousin) crossed to England and was promised the succession to the Crown.

There is no reason to doubt the story. Edward was childless, and the nearest heir of the English line was a son of Edmund Ironside, Edward the Exile, who had lived in Hungary since early childhood and was no more than a name to the English. Godwine's successful return, however, and the increasing power of his son Harold after his death in 1053, made it certain that the English would not tamely accept William. They had seen too much of Normans, and had a strong case for denying Edward's right to appoint his successor.

HAROLD

As Edward's grasp of affairs relaxed, Harold and his brothers Tostig, Gyrth, and Leofwine gradually extended their hold on England till only Mercia remained under an earl of a different

*Harold goes hunting with hawk **and belled hounds** (Bayeux Tapestry)*

The death of Edward the Confessor: Edward commends the kingdom to Harold: Queen Edith, Harold's sister, weeps (Bayeux Tapestry)

family. If the House of Godwine had remained united, it is possible that the Battle of Hastings would have had a different ending and that Wessex would have given a second royal House to England. Towards the end of Edward's reign, however, there was a turn of events which was to prove disastrous for Harold. In 1065 his brother Tostig, who had been for ten years Earl of Northumbria, was expelled by a rebellion in favour of Morcar, brother of Earl Edwin of Mercia. Harold advised the King and Witan to accept the situation rather than launch a civil war against the northern earls, and in doing so he made a bitter personal enemy of Tostig. Banished from the kingdom, Tostig retired to plot revenge; and the whole affair weakened the House of Godwine and strengthened its only competitor.

It was about this time, and probably in the previous year, that something else happened which made little stir at the moment but had important consequences. According to the Norman story, Harold arrived in Normandy on an errand from Edward to William. More probably he was cast ashore there by bad weather, but in any case he was seized by the local baron and then by the Duke. It was a great stroke of luck for William. He knew that Harold was the most powerful man in England, and the only serious rival for the Throne which he coveted. He kept Harold for some time as an honoured but unwilling guest, taking him on campaigns in which the Englishman acquitted himself well, and eventually offered him an oath of homage as the price of freedom. Harold took the oath, binding himself to be William's 'man' and support his claim to England. He had little choice, since Edward was near his end and refusal would have meant remaining hostage in Normandy while William dealt with a leaderless England. William let him go, hoping he would keep his oath but now ready to brand him perjurer before the whole of Christendom if he did not.

Early in January 1066 Edward died, after commending the kingdom to Harold. There was an heir of the royal

5

House, Edgar the Atheling (son of Edward the Exile); but he was only a child of nine, while Harold had already proved his capacity as war-leader and had the personal loyalty of at least half the English. The nobles and bishops of the Witan were still assembled for the regular Christmas gathering, and the next day they confirmed Harold as king and crowned him. The haste shows that they expected trouble from Normandy, and were anxious to present William with an accomplished fact before he had time to protest. There is no evidence that Edwin or Morcar raised any objection, but Harold was rightly doubtful of the loyalty of the North. One of his first acts was to travel there to show himself and secure allegiance.

THE INVASIONS OF 1066

William probably half-expected this development. He knew Harold for a man of great spirit who could not easily submit to serve another, much less tamely surrender England against the will of the English. The broken oath, however, gave him a fine excuse to cloak his intended aggression with an appearance of righteousness and brought him the papal blessing. He lost no time in making ready, setting the shipwrights and armourers to work to build and equip an invasion fleet, while he called on the Normans to help him and sent out agents to attract soldiers of fortune from all over Northern France with promises of pay and plunder. He could not strike at once, for six

6

months at least were needed to build sufficient vessels.

In May the detestable Tostig put in an appearance, raiding by sea up the south and east coasts and landing in Lincolnshire to ravage. The Northern Earls beat him off without difficulty, and he retired to prepare another attempt with much larger forces.

By midsummer the main threat in the South was developing fast, and Harold prepared to meet it. Ships were called out to patrol between the Isle of Wight and the Straits of Dover, and Harold himself with his housecarles took post in Sussex while the local fyrd mustered behind him. Condemned to a waiting role, he could do no more. He had not the shipping or the force for a spoiling attack across the Channel against the invasion fleet. But the English forces were not organised to stand idle for months. As time dragged

on and there was still no sign of William, their provisions ran out and many were urgently needed at home to get in the harvest. After the first week of September Harold's host disintegrated. The ships, which had suffered from storms in August and were out of supplies, had to be sent round to London to refit, and the fyrd could no longer be held together.

The South then lay open to invasion—at the very moment when Tostig and King Harold Hardrada of Norway attacked the North. On September 15th Harold had word of this new threat, and started north with such force as he could muster to meet it. He had no alternative: five days later the Norwegians defeated the Northern Earls at Fulford, near York, and after this the Northumbrians (who had never really accepted Harold) agreed to join Hardrada and march south.

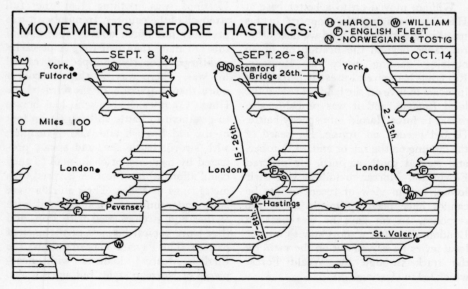

Harold could not face William with a victorious enemy at his back: his only hope was to strike at the one enemy within his reach, and then double on his tracks before the other landed.

With his amazing capacity for forced marches, Harold reached Yorkshire and challenged the Norwegians to immediate battle on the 25th. At Stamford Bridge he utterly routed them. Hardrada and Tostig both fell, and we are told that 24 ships were sufficient to carry off the survivors of a host which had arrived in 300. The rest had gained for themselves no more than 'six feet of English earth', but they had given William the chance to unload his crowded and vulnerable transports on a completely undefended coast. When the Norman fleet set sail on the 27th., and landed the next day at Pevensey, Harold was far away and the English ships were still in London River.

William moved on to a better base at Hastings, ravaging the country in his usual ruthless manner, and we hear of no resistance beyond the beating off of an outlying raiding party at Romney. Ravaging had several uses: it helped the invaders to 'live off the land', it cowed the local English, and it was probably also meant to force Harold into speedy battle. Harold needed no urging. He heard of the landing on the 1st. or 2nd. of October, and started south at once. He ordered Edwin and Morcar to follow with their forces, but in view of recent events he cannot have been optimistic about the response. In six days he was back in London, and after a short stay to muster local levies he moved out on the 11th. by the track through the Weald Forest which led to Hastings.

The Hastings district then formed a peninsula cut off to east and west by tidal marshes, and three days marching brought Harold to the point where the road left the forest and crossed the narrow neck of rising land at some six miles distance from the little port. It was the obvious place for a stand, since as long as he held it the Normans were bottled in the peninsula; and if he could maintain the position while his ships sailed round to the enemy rear there was a fair chance of final victory. He could not, however, risk a direct attack on the Normans. He had himself ridden in war with William's knights, and he knew well enough that English infantry tactics could only stand up to them in a firm defensive line on a well-chosen position.

THE BATTLE OF HASTINGS

The force which Harold mustered at Hastings was nothing like the full strength of the country. In number it was probably not much above 7000, and of this not more than half were housecarles and thegns properly equipped and trained for war. There was no time to collect more than a fraction of the fyrd of the Home Counties. Those who had horses to get them to battle still fought on foot in the old English and Viking manner, with sword, battle-axe, and spear, protected by hauberks of chain-mail (if they could afford it) or of leather covered with metal rings or scales. Their shields were large and round, of wood covered with leather and strengthened with iron, and they wore conical helmets of the ancient pattern. The Bayeux Tapestry shows the English wearing helmets with nose-pieces of Norman style; but since it also

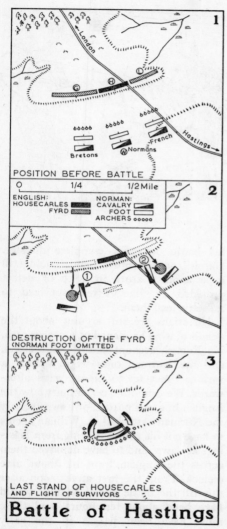

1

Position before battle

O 1/4 1/2 Mile

ENGLISH:
HOUSECARLES
FYRD

NORMAN:
CAVALRY
FOOT
ARCHERS ooooo

London

Hastings →

French

Normans

Bretons

2

DESTRUCTION OF THE FYRD
(NORMAN FOOT OMITTED)

3

LAST STAND OF HOUSECARLES
AND FLIGHT OF SURVIVORS

Battle of Hastings

short trousers: they seem rather to have been slit fore and aft for ease of movement.

The fyrd, apart from the thegns who led them, relied mainly on the spear and had little body armour. A few had short bows, but not enough to affect the battle, and otherwise their only missiles were light javelins and throwing clubs.

The 'Norman' numbers were probably about the same, but the make-up of their force was entirely different. At least half of it was not Norman, being knights and soldiers of fortune from Brittany, Flanders, and other parts of France. Its backbone was the mailed cavalry, armoured much like the English thegns except for differences of shield and helmet, but trained to charge home with all the weight of horse and rider and to fight with lance, sword, and mace from horseback. The infantry outnumbered these, but were far less important. They had, however, a large number of archers armed with the old Viking short bow which was deadly up to about fifty yards, and this could be used with effect to shake a defensive front in preparation for the charge.

When Harold took up his position on the low ridge where Battle Abbey now stands, William had every reason to accept the challenge without delay. Storms or the English ships might cut him off from Normandy, and the Hastings district could not long supply his army. Inactivity would have been not only pointless but bad for the morale of his troops, while it would allow Harold's reinforcement by the fyrd still mustering behind him. William therefore struck at once, in full knowledge that he must win

gives most of them the kite-shaped shields which were designed specially for use on horseback, it may be wrong on both counts. It is probably also mistaken in making its hauberks end in a pair of

9

Above: Charge of Norman cavalry; one rider has his lance couched, another hurls his lance from a distance; the English also throw spears and a club

Below: Norman archers; one is armoured like a knight and holds a sheaf of arrows in his bow hand for rapid shooting (Bayeux Tapestry)

his battle or suffer complete disaster. Harold, on the other hand, could still raise another army in spite of defeat provided he, like Alfred, survived to rally and lead them.

Historians are still arguing about the details of what happened on October 14th. No English account of the battle exists, and the Norman ones were written at various times up to ninety years afterwards. We cannot be certain just how the English line was posted, or how precisely the Normans attacked it. William seems to have got his troops moving from Hastings at dawn, and to have deployed them across the English front by about nine o'clock. From the first attack soon after this till the battle ended at dusk would have been about ten hours, and there must have been pauses in the early stages while both sides got their breath back and prepared for the next onslaught.

It seems that William drew up his force in three divisions, each containing archers, mailed infantry, and knights, with his Normans in the centre. Attacks with archery alone made little impression, since the short bow could not pierce the Saxon shield, and onslaughts by infantry and cavalry in turn failed to break the English line. The great two-handed axes of the housecarles made notable havoc, and a shower of javelins, throwing-clubs, and small throwing-axes met the enemy at close quarters. The attacking left wing recoiled, and it seems that the fyrd on the English right broke its ranks to chase them down the slope, only to be caught in confusion by a charge of cavalry and ridden down in the open.

Another heavy general attack still failed to break through, but Harold's brothers Gyrth and Leofwine were killed in the mêleé. It was after this that the famous incident of the 'feigned flight' took place. Some have doubted whether this really was a planned ruse, but there seems no reason why such a trick should not have been arranged during a pause in the fighting. Norman attackers pressed to the English line and then hastily retreated, drawing most of the fyrd after them down the hill to their doom.

Long after this the Saxon centre held out, against charges and against a close-range dropping archery to which it could make no reply. Only as night was drawing near did the front at last waver, and allow the knights to break in and complete the rout. Harold was hewn down beneath his standards, and only a remnant fought its way out over broken ground northwards to the shelter of the forest. The legend that Harold was killed, or mortally wounded, by an arrow in the eye probably comes from a misreading of the Bayeux Tapestry.

The Saxon housecarles defend themselves with axe and sword; note the round shield with boss and rim (Bayeux Tapestry)

Harold, last of the Saxon kings, died in the best tradition of his race, fighting to the end in what had become a hopeless struggle. It was no lack of courage, or vigour, or generalship which brought disaster: it was the result of an isolated and obsolete military system. Disaster it certainly was, for none of the Earls of Godwine's line were left to rally another army against William, and most of the trained fighting men of Southern England were dead. The spirit of resistance was not quenched, but without leadership and organisation it could not alter the verdict of this one day's work.

WILLIAM BECOMES KING

After a few days rest William moved on

London, which must be taken before he could feel secure. Inside it was the child Edgar the Atheling, and some of the Witan who declared him king. London was strongly walled and populous, well able to defend itself against assault, and in determined hands it could have become a rallying point for English resistance. William did not, however, trust his army to Harold's direct route through the woods and thickets of the Weald where it could have been easily ambushed as it trailed along the narrow track. Instead he skirted along the coast to Romney, where he revenged himself for the previous resistance, and thence to Dover, where he spent a week erecting an earthwork castle. From Dover the old Roman road ran straight across the open uplands of the chalk to Canterbury, and thence to London.

Illness delayed him some time at Canterbury, and then he pushed on to the capital. Not till he was within reach of London Bridge was any resistance offered, and this was easily brushed aside. He could not capture the bridge, however, and he had to content himself with burning Southwark and then ravaging a wide belt of country along the south of the Thames until he found a suitable crossing at Wallingford. Thence he continued beneath the Chilterns to Little Berkhampstead, clearly intending to isolate and starve London into surrender. By that time the magnates in the city, who had watched his progress with the terrified inaction of rabbits, at last made up their minds and surrendered. Edwin and Morcar, the Archbishop of York, Bishop Wulfstan of Worcester, and the leading Londoners, swore fealty and

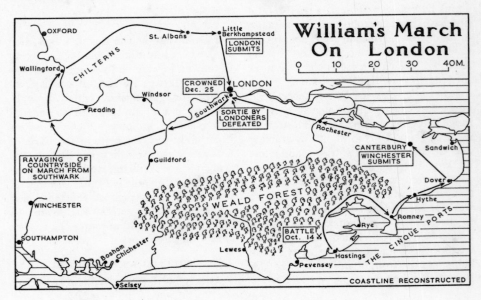

The surrender of London

gave hostages. This did not, however, prevent the Normans continuing their ravage along the road to London. On Christmas Day William was duly crowned at Westminster, and the main task of conquest was over. Scattered and unorganised resistance was still to come, but with the sole result of making William and his Normans more absolute masters of the country.

In all the long history of the Danish Wars, there had been nothing like it. Campaigns had dragged on for years, and had mostly ended in compromise or indecision. Even Canute's conquest had only succeeded with the untimely death of Edmund Ironside after the interminable wars of Ethelred's reign. Besides the impact of Norman cavalry in open warfare, which explains much, the English lack of fortresses or willingness to defend them is striking. Dover,

Canterbury, Winchester, surrendered without a blow, and even London submitted rather than stand a siege. The burh organisation of Alfred's time, which would have held up the invader and perhaps prolonged the war till he was forced to come to terms, seems to have perished of neglect in the years of peace. When both sides fought on foot, it was generally possible for the king to get away from a lost battle and live to fight another day, but Hastings had removed all the adults of the royal House at one blow.

Canute had been content to accept England much as he found it, but William now had the opportunity as well as the desire to remodel it on his own terms. William had now to perform the circus feat of riding two horses, Normandy and England, and the task would be easier if England conformed to the sys-

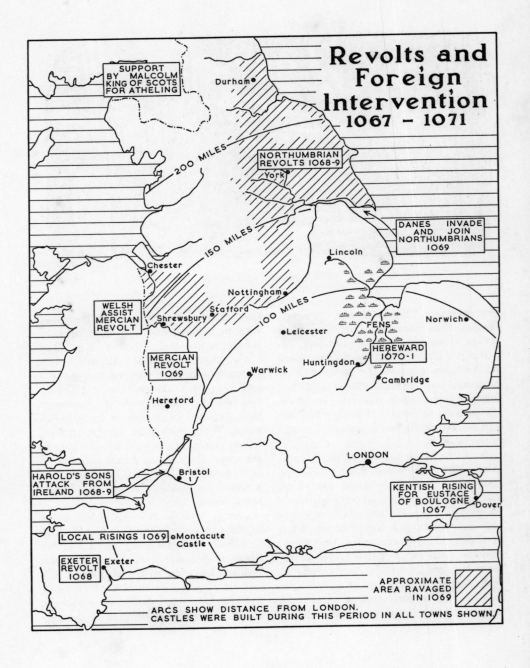

Revolts and Foreign Intervention 1067 – 1071

SUPPORT BY MALCOLM KING OF SCOTS FOR ATHELING

Durham

200 MILES

NORTHUMBRIAN REVOLTS 1068-9

York

150 MILES

DANES INVADE AND JOIN NORTHUMBRIANS 1069

Chester

Lincoln

Nottingham

100 MILES

WELSH ASSIST MERCIAN REVOLT

Shrewsbury

Stafford

Leicester

FENS

Norwich

MERCIAN REVOLT 1069

Warwick

Huntingdon

HEREWARD 1070-1

Hereford

Cambridge

LONDON

HAROLD'S SONS ATTACK FROM IRELAND 1068-9

Bristol

KENTISH RISING FOR EUSTACE OF BOULOGNE 1067

Dover

LOCAL RISINGS 1069

Montacute Castle

EXETER REVOLT 1068

Exeter

APPROXIMATE AREA RAVAGED IN 1069

ARCS SHOW DISTANCE FROM LONDON.
CASTLES WERE BUILT DURING THIS PERIOD IN ALL TOWNS SHOWN.

tem he knew in Normandy. He could not, like Canute, settle permanently in England and rule his other realm by deputy from a distance; the ducal power depended too much on personal supervision.

THE ENGLISH REBELLIONS

The new king's first acts were to raise a general Danegeld in England, impose fines on those who had helped Harold, and seize the lands of the Englishmen killed at Hastings. He at once began a castle inside the walls of London, to secure his hold on that vital city. Within three months he felt safe enough to cross to Normandy, and remained there till the end of the year. He took with him as a precaution those Englishmen who might have led a revolt in his absence, and in fact there was no trouble of any importance while he was away. Not till he came back and began in 1068 to enforce his authority in the remoter parts of the country was there any opposition, and then it was not national. It is remarkable that within two years of Hastings he was able to call out the English fyrd to help him against English rebels, and that on the whole it served him loyally.

In 1068 Harold's (illegitimate) sons roused Exeter to shut its gates against William, and the city stood an eighteen day siege before it surrendered on terms. The ringleaders escaped to Ireland, but the place was treated with surprising lenience. A castle was built inside the walls, and thenceforth it gave no more trouble.

More dangerous was the rising of the North, stirred up by Edwin and Morcar after they tired of their practical captivity at William's court and escaped to raise the men of their earldoms. On William's approach, however, their forces melted away and they submitted once more. Castles were built in York, Warwick, Nottingham, Lincoln, Huntingdon, and Cambridge, and Normans were settled in Leicester. Thinking the business over, William paid off his hired troops and retired south; but the ravages by his deputy in Northumbria drove the recalcitrant northerners to further rebellion. At the beginning of 1069 they surprised and slaughtered the deputy and his retinue at Durham, and tried to take the new castle at York. William had to raise the siege and build a second castle to control the northern capital.

Meanwhile Harold's sons were making futile raids on the West from bases in Ireland, and later in the year Sweyn of Denmark accepted a Northumbrian offer of the Crown and sent a fleet to assist against William. With Danish help York was taken, and its Norman garrison killed after they had fired the town. This was the moment for the English to rise, had there been any real national leadership and will to resist, but in fact nothing happened but a few scattered and feeble attacks on new castles in Mercia and the South-West. William had had enough, and after retaking York and getting rid of the Danes he began the dreadful episode of the 'harrying of the North'. In Yorkshire villages went up in flames, and their inhabitants were slaughtered. North of Tees there was similar destruction, though the people had enough warning to escape across the Tyne, and the shires of Derby, Stafford, and Chester were likewise ravaged.

The effect was both immediate and long-lasting. Those Yorkshiremen who

The harrying of the North

survived made no further attempt at rebellion, and for long afterwards the nettle-grown sites of former villages gave a silent warning. Durham, which had suffered less severely, did indeed rise again in 1080 against its Norman earl-bishop, and suffered further devastation.

The heroic stand of the Lincolnshire thegn Hereward in the Isle of Ely in 1071 marked the last dying spark of English independence; and in 1075 William relied on the fyrd to deal with a rising of a few dissatisfied Norman barons.

The result of these struggles, futile as they were, was to wipe out what remained of the English landowning class after Hastings. By 1075 the last of the English earls, Waltheof, was executed for complicity with the rebels of that year; and the rebellions had given William an excuse to confiscate the property of nearly every thegn of importance who had not already lost life or lands through the battles of 1066. By the time of Doomsday Book there remained only two

Englishmen holding large estates as tenants-in-chief, and the thegns in general, if not completely dispossessed, had been reduced to petty freeholders. This was a great advantage to William, since it left him free to regrant the land to his own followers and impose on the country a propertied ruling class which was solidly Norman. Many of the disinherited, seeing no future in England, moved to Scotland or to the Continent, and a considerable number entered the Varangian Guard of the Emperors of Constantinople.

NORMAN FEUDALISM

The whole basis of Norman rule in England was also affected. At first William had claimed simply to be the true heir of Edward the Confessor, and to have recovered his rightful throne from the 'usurper' Harold. On this theory he would be obliged to accept English law and institutions, and to co-operate with and rule through all those

English magnates and officials who had not actually assisted Harold in the 'rebellion' of Hastings. To begin with, this seems to have been his intention. There was at first no clean sweep of English earls, bishops, and sheriffs, and leading English notables continued to sit in his Great Council as previously in the Witan. But the eclipse of the English earls and thegns changed the whole picture. From 1071 onwards Englishmen disappear from prominent positions in Church and State. What might have been a genuine Anglo-Norman partnership became instead a Norman domination of a conquered race.

William had it both ways. As Edward's heir he took over the great taxing and law-making powers of English kings, the ancient prestige of the Crown, and as much of the English system of government as he found convenient: but he grafted on to this a Norman feudal ruling class, the feudal principle of the king as universal landlord, and the direct control of the Church which had been the prerogative of Norman dukes.

Norman feudalism, as imposed in England, was an excellent device for ensuring the hold of a small alien military aristocracy over an immensely larger population of conquered English. Less than two hundred 'barons', mainly of those leading Norman families who had supported William in 1066, received the bulk of the estates confiscated from English landowners. With this land they took over the old Saxon obligations to the king, and also the duty of providing a fixed number of knights trained and equipped for cavalry service. Whether the baron endowed his knights with land

as sub-tenants, or simply maintained them in his household, was his own affair. At first most of them were only retainers of no great social standing, though the practice of giving them land-grants soon became general and increased their independence and importance.

In this way the king could call out over four thousand cavalry—more than he had at Hastings—and in addition the bishoprics and larger abbeys were now obliged to find some eight hundred more on account of their estates. In war-time the period of service seems to have been two months, and in peace forty days per year of castle-guard or escort duty.

The chief danger of continental feudalism—the defiance of the king by barons backed by their retainers—could not be a serious threat in England so long as the Norman minority was obliged to hold together against the English. In France a man's loyalty was to his immediate overlord alone, and barons claimed a right to conduct private wars against each other. William was not having this in England. The famous 'Oath of Salisbury' of 1086, by which all the more important sub-tenants swore personal fidelity to the king, stressed the old Saxon principle that loyalty to a lord could not cut across the duty of all men to the monarch; and this remained a part of the English law.

The estates of the greater landowners were scattered all over the country. It is not now believed that William did this of set purpose, but rather that it arose through the piecemeal confiscations after 1066 and the already scattered estates of Saxon notables which the barons took over. It did, however, have the effect of preventing great blocks of territory developing into practically independent units, as Normandy itself had done in France. On the contrary, it obliged the great landowners to travel and to be interested in the affairs of the whole country, instead of taking a purely local view. Only on the borders, where defence against Welsh or Scots required particularly powerful barons, did William permit the existence of solid earldoms like those of Durham, Chester, Shrewsbury, and (for a time) Hereford.

The great majority of the land in England was now held from the king by military service, and as sub-tenants in turn received estates there developed that complicated and in detail highly unsystematic arrangement called the 'Feudal System'. The basic principle was that all land was held in return for some sort of service. Barons (including the bishops and greater abbots) owed 'suit of court' as well as knight-service. They attended the three annual meetings of the Great Council, and any emergency meeting, to discuss and advise on measures the king proposed and to settle disputes amongst themselves. Similarly the sub-tenants attended the baron's court at the chief castle of the barony or 'honour', and at the bottom of the scale the villein tenants were bound to appear at the court of the manor. At each step there were payments called 'reliefs' to the immediate overlord for taking up an inheritance, and 'aids' for meeting unusual expenses, and the overlord had the right to take the profits of an estate while the heir was a minor or to find a husband for an heiress or widow.

Grave complications set in if tenants came to hold of several lords, or if the

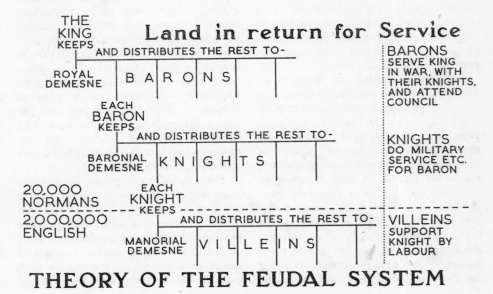

THEORY OF THE FEUDAL SYSTEM

18

'knight's fee' charged with producing one knight for service became split among many owners. Knights might grow too old to fight, and by the end of the century the practice of paying a 'scutage' of twenty shillings or two marks in place of military service was already creeping in. Under William, however, the new system was still comparatively straightforward.

Some land was held by service of a different nature. The tenure called 'Frankalmoign' or 'free alms' might involve no other obligation than that of praying for the soul of the grantor and his kinsmen, and 'Sergeanty' allowed the holding of fiefs by the royal huntsmen, goldsmiths, cooks, and similar craftsmen. Some English freeholders survived the confiscations, especially in the Danelaw, and they were fitted loosely into the system as freemen or socagers owing only money and small non-menial services.

As the new ruling class displaced the Saxon magnates and landlords, they took over also their place in the Church and the pre-feudal offices surviving from Saxon times. William never appointed an Englishman as bishop: as sees became vacant he filled them with Normans or other continentals, and the same was true of the important abbeys. By the end of his reign there were only two English bishops, and two major abbots, surviving from before 1066. The high officials of the royal household, and the sheriffs who were the king's deputies in the shires, were also nearly all Normans.

ROYAL GOVERNMENT

Apart from its lack of feudal organisation, Saxon England had had a much more regular and developed system of government than Normandy. Its laws were mostly codified (which Norman custom was not) and it had the sealed royal writ by which the king sent his orders to the sheriffs to be passed on to the freeholders in the shire court. In the danegeld (or by this time simply 'geld') the king had a simple and efficient means of raising a land-tax from the whole country, and his Household was more elaborate and better provided with clerks. William kept all this, only replacing English officials with Normans, with the result that in England his authority was more absolute and effective even than in Normandy. With the addition of feudal organisation and the king's new position as universal landlord it gave him the strongest monarchy in Western Europe, and the system evolved by Saxon genius was used to rivet the foreign yoke more firmly on English necks. What that depressed and now inarticulate race thought of it all we do not hear, but we can well guess.

William was a great one for enforcing the law, but like all Norman kings he changed it little. In general he accepted the 'laws of Edward the Confessor' as they stood. There was no question of Norman law replacing English, for it was much less developed. The only changes he thought fit to make were the separation of Church legal business from the shire court, the introduction of a special protection for Normans and other foreigners against murder, and the replacement of the death penalty by loss of limb. (Forest Law was a separate matter, which will be dealt with later). In Saxon times the bishop had sat with the sheriff in the shire court, and offences against Church law had been tried there alongside secular business. In accord with the normal arrangement of the time on the Continent, William gave the Church its own courts (though the bishop rather oddly also continued for some time to sit with the sheriff). If a man were found murdered, and the slayer could not be produced, the men of the Hundred must either prove that the dead man was English or pay a heavy collective fine which (like Saxon wergild) went partly to the king and partly to the dead man's relations. The only definitely Norman procedure introduced was Trial by Battle between accuser and accused in criminal cases, and even then Englishmen (as distinct from Normans) were not compelled to undergo it.

In due course Henry I restored capital punishment, and made new laws to protect the currency and fix standard measures, but Norman legislation amounted to very little. More important in the long run was the development of the jury in royal courts under Henry I and particularly under Henry II, with the issue of royal writs to remove a case from feudal courts to those of the shire. The origins of the English jury system are still disputed. The Normans had been familiar with juries in France as a convenient device for getting at local facts, and as such William used them in the Doomsday Survey; but already in late Saxon times they had operated, in Lincolnshire at least, to declare guilt or innocence in criminal cases. If the Normans did not introduce them to England, they used them frequently to decide disputes over land; and once their use was well-established it was natural, as the

Ordeal fell into disfavour, to extend it to criminal verdicts.

With two separate systems of justice, royal and feudal, there was bound to be much conflict (since the right to try cases meant the right to collect fines and forfeitures). Already under Henry I, however, royal lawyers were finding means to transfer business from the feudal courts. One thing which must have borne hardly on the English was the fact that henceforth for centuries laws were written, if at all, in Latin and cases conducted in Norman-French—a state of affairs highly satisfactory to the new rising legal fraternity.

In revenue, as in other matters, William made the best both of old English and new feudal sources. A large sum was raised from the 'farm' of the shires—a money composition for the ancient food-rents and other rights of the Crown—and there was always the geld on land whenever something more was needed. Profits from the royal courts were also valuable. Besides these came the mass of new feudal dues and 'incidents': reliefs, the profits of the estates of minors and of vacant sees and abbeys, and the tallage collected at will from royal boroughs and tenants on the king's demesne. When scutage in due course came to be taken in place of armed service, it developed into something like another regular tax. The Norman kings were very comfortably off for money; and so were the feudal ruling class, for they could pass on to their tenants most of what they had to pay the king. The burden fell, as usual in ancient times, upon those lowest in the scale and least able to bear it.

One purely Norman branch of law was imposed in England—the special Law of the Forest. English kings had had hunting preserves, but the extent and nature of the new law was something quite different. The Norman kings were all great hunters, since the sport was their chief relaxation from the formality and business of their lives, and as they moved much about the country they selected suitable areas at their own will and declared them 'forest'. The term did not necessarily mean woodland: great stretches of open moor were included, and some villages with their arable fields were found in 'forest' areas. It was simply a legal word for land under Forest Law, and the making of the New Forest, for example, did not involve planting the trees (though in this case it did mean destroying villages). Within the forest bounds none might hunt the deer or boar, or cut down the trees and thickets which sheltered and fed them. Even lesser animals like the rabbit might only be taken by those to whom the king granted 'right of warren', and this was unlikely to include the peasantry.

The king's pleasure took no account of the needs of the population in 'forest' areas. The villager who had previously eked out his diet with rabbits for the pot and supplied his fire or mended his cottage with wood from the 'waste' was now strictly forbidden to do either. Nor could new land be cleared for crops. When, by later Norman times, the forest included well over a quarter of the whole country, this was a grievous burden. Special verderer's courts were set up to enforce the drastic penalties, and to see that all dogs in the bounds were 'lawed'

by having three claws from each foot chopped off to disable them from chasing the king's animals. For a villein to kill deer was death, and a freeman who resisted a verderer lost both freedom and possessions. Inevitably the law was broken wholesale, in spite of its vicious penalties, as similar laws against poaching were defied in the early nineteenth century; and as population grew, encroachment on the woodlands was inevitable. Sometimes this was done by paying for royal licence, and sometimes simply by going ahead and paying the fine in due course. In the Middle Ages legal restrictions often served much more as a source of revenue through collecting fines for their breach than as a means of stopping people doing what they were in fact going to do anyway.

Forest Law was bad law, since the benefit the king got from it was far less than the harm it did to many thousands of his subjects. Such laws have always led to disrespect for authority in general, and its existence is a blot on the Norman reputation for statesmanship.

THE CHURCH

The effect of the Conquest upon the Church in England was profound. Its organisation was tightened up and brought more directly under royal control, its higher ranks were 'Normanised' like the lay nobility, and it was opened to the influence of the new reform movement which at this time was sweeping the Continent. William's attitude was quite forthright: he was a good churchman, and glad to see imposed on the Church the order and discipline which he loved. But he would not brook any outside interference in his kingdom which would diminish his own authority. So far as reform went, he was happy to co-operate with a reforming Papacy; but there was to be no question of direct papal control, much less of the claims to dominion over kings which some popes were now beginning hopefully to assert.

The English kings had always had a marked respect for the Papacy, and William's attitude was more, not less, independent. He would allow no pope to be recognised, or to take action, in England without his approval, and no bishop to go to Rome without his permission even at the pope's summons. Canons of the English Church were subject to his veto, and there was to be no excommunication of his ministers or barons without his leave. Having made this clear, he encouraged the work of internal reform. In this connection his happiest and most important appointment was Lanfranc, a famous Italian scholar who had been abbot of his monastery at Caen, to be Archbishop of Canterbury in 1070.

Death or deposition removed all but three of the English bishops by that year, and William filled their places mostly with clerks from his own chancery—men he could depend on for personal loyalty. As the English abbots died, their places too were filled with Normans or others from the Continent at Lanfranc's suggestion. Most of them were good men, though some expressed too liberally that typical Norman arrogance and contempt for all things English. They may have thought that their predecessors in office were 'yokels' and 'uncouth simpletons', but they need not have said so.

Nor was it kindly to cross off the Church calendar the local saints whom the English had venerated for centuries, or, as at St. Albans, to break up the monuments of previous abbots. Tact was not a Norman virtue. When Thurstan at Glastonbury hunted his monks through the church with archers and slaughtered some of them at the altar because they objected to his new-fangled methods of chanting, he went too far even for Norman ideas of the abbot's duties and was suspended. Such incidents, however, were exceptional, and were no part of Lanfranc's scheme.

In 1072 the archbishop held the first of a series of Church Councils, in which the work of reform was carried through. The increased authority of the bishop under the new order required that sees in remote villages should be moved to county towns, and consequently cathedrals were transferred from Lichfield, Selsey, Sherborne, and Dorchester-on-Thames to Chester, Chichester, Old Sarum, and Lincoln. The old East Anglian see of Elmham moved to Thetford, and later to Norwich.

The peculiar English institution of the Cathedral Monastery, dating from the reforms of Dunstan, was however respected. In these foundations (at Canterbury, Winchester, Worcester, and Sherborne) monks took the place of canons in the services of the cathedral choir, and the bishop was also abbot of the House. The first Norman bishop of Winchester did indeed try to get rid of his monks, but Lanfranc's appointment came in time to save them. He approved the idea, and with papal blessing it was extended further. At Rochester and Durham re-

Norman Sees

MONASTERY CATHEDRALS-■ EARLIER SITES INDICATED.

CARLISLE 1133

DURHAM ■

YORK

ARCHBISHRICS OF: YORK CANTERBURY

BANGOR

ST. ASAPH

CHESTER

Lichfield

Elmham

NORWICH

Thetford

ELY 1109

HEREFORD

ST. DAVIDS

WORCESTER

LLANDAFF

Dorchester

LONDON

ROC HES TER

CANTER BURY

BATH

Wells

SALISBURY

WINCHESTER

CHICHESTER

Crediton

Sherborne

Selsey

EXETER

0   50   100 Mls.

founded monasteries were attached to the cathedrals, and later under Anselm the monks of Ely were given a bishop.

The separation of the Church courts from those of the shire meant freedom to develop and administer Canon Law independently of the law of the land, in concert with the new continental re-forms. Hence in 1076 a determined effort was made to compel the clergy to remain unmarried. Previously, as in the Eastern Orthodox Churches to this day, bishops had been celibate but ordinary parish clergy could marry before ordination. But the reforming Pope Hildebrand (Gregory VII, 1073–85) was determined to force celibacy on all in priest's orders. Canons of the English Church in this year, following those of Rome, decreed that no more married men were to be ordained, or existing bachelor priests to marry. Those already married were allowed to keep their wives, but it was intended that in a generation the whole clergy should be single. Like most mediaeval legislation, this proved in practice hard to enforce. A century later there were still married priests, and in some cases churches were passing from father to son by inheritance.

No attempt was made, however, to alter the old English arrangement by which parish churches were regarded as belonging to the landowners whose predecessors had founded them, with the right to appoint the parson and receive part of the tithe income. To disturb this would have been to tamper with the property rights of the feudal ruling class, the king included, and the Church was not independent enough for this. The rather odd practice of lay patronage and advowson in fact survives, in a modified form, to this day, and in early mediaeval times the transference of such rights to a monastery was a common means of endowment.

The new Church courts, held locally by Archdeacons who for the first time become important figures, dealt with offences against the Church, against individual churches or churchmen, or against morality in matters covered by Canon but not by ordinary law. They also took cases arising over marriages or wills, like the modern court of Probate and Divorce. Laymen came under Church jurisdiction in such matters, but clergy had to submit to lay courts in disputes over property (including advowson) or matters of the Forest Law. If a layman refused to appear in a Church court he would be excommunicated, and if this had no effect a royal writ would be obtained instructing the sheriff to arrest him and hand him over. Under William we do not hear of conflict arising between the two parallel sets of courts and law, because his authority over both was final. But later on, when the Church grew more powerful and independent, complications were inevitable.

MONASTERIES

The Conquest was followed by an immense revival and expansion of the monastic life in England, though far more of this was due to the reforms which arose at this period on the Continent than to the Normans themselves. The English monasteries in 1066 were by no means as black as Norman critics painted them, but undoubtedly the effect of Dunstan's reforms a century earlier was wearing off. There were some three dozen of them, all independent Benedictine or 'black monk' houses, and between them they had revenues which amounted in Doomsday Book to about a sixth of the income of the whole kingdom. The effects of the Viking wars in blotting out the venerable northern monasteries had never been repaired. There was only one north of Trent, and that on the river at Burton; and all Lincolnshire and East Anglia (apart from the Fens) had only two. Even in the south, whole shires like Sussex and Cornwall had none at all.

Isolation had been their chief drawback. They had none of the splendid buildings now rising in France, and showed little of the learning and vigour which helped to make this period the great age of the continental monasteries. To the Normans they appeared backward and provincial, content with unenterprising respectability.

Politically, too, they were suspect. Their monks came mostly from the Saxon landowning families, their abbots from the nobility, and their sympathies were wholly English. Some abbots had actively opposed the Conqueror, and had fled or been deposed. The rest, now fitted into the feudal system and owing knight-service for their lands, were from every Norman point of view better replaced. Fortunately Lanfranc, as William's instrument in this process, knew how to achieve results by considerate dealing instead of Norman harshness. There was no clean sweep, but as abbots and monks died their places were taken by Normans. Only Worcester and Peterborough among the greater houses long preserved an English majority.

The result was a tightening up of the observance of the Rule of St. Benedict, especially in matters such as silence, diet restriction, and the ban on personal property which were the first to suffer in lax times, and the introduction of the elaborate services and chanting now popular on the Continent. New buildings on the grand scale were put in hand, beginning with a massive church, and Latin became the language of the new learning and, to some extent, of daily life. Numbers grew rapidly—a sign of vigour in a period of expansion, but a danger to standards if enthusiasm cooled. New houses also were founded, like

William's great thank-offering foundation at Battle, and staffed with monks imported direct from France.

One result, however, was less fortunate. The endowment of French monasteries with manors in England led to the widespread growth of 'cells' or 'granges', where a few monks from across the Channel lived to administer the estate. These little houses had neither the buildings nor the numbers for a proper community life, and their occupants were too much preoccupied with everyday business. They were a danger to monastic standards, and the first to fall into decline. Not all were foreign-owned: some were once independent abbeys which had fallen on evil days and been attached to another house, and some had been founded with the intention, never fulfilled, of achieving sufficient numbers for independence.

While the Conquest Normanised most of the monasteries and doubled the number of monks, it also stimulated to a notable revival those which did not at first come under Norman control. Worcester, where the venerable if unlearned Wulfstan remained bishop-abbot till his death in 1095, and nearby Evesham under Abbot Ethelwig, also grew in numbers till they were able to send out colonies of monks to begin the great rebirth of monasticism in the North. They resettled and rebuilt the ruins at Jarrow, Wearmouth, and Whitby, and in due course monks from these new centres restored the houses at Durham and York. Recruits came from the South, perhaps to escape Norman abbots, and the Benedictine foundations of Northumbria long remained English rather than Norman.

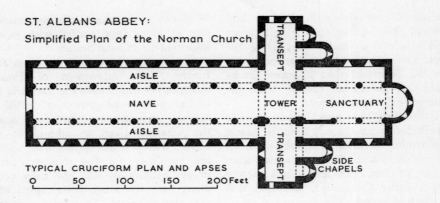

ST. ALBANS ABBEY:
Simplified Plan of the Norman Church

TRANSEPT

AISLE

NAVE   TOWER   SANCTUARY

AISLE

TRANSEPT

SIDE
CHAPELS

TYPICAL CRUCIFORM PLAN AND APSES

0   50   100   150   200 Feet

NORMAN CHURCHES*

Architecture was probably the only art in which the Normans were more advanced than the English, and this they had recently learnt from the Romanesque buildings of Northern France. The few remaining examples of Saxon work do not represent the best the pre-Conquest English could do: they are mostly in small and remote places, and of Saxon cathedrals nothing apart from some ruins at Elmham remains above ground. Nevertheless, there is no doubt that Norman work was superior in solidity and design. The break here was complete, for the Normans took no account of Saxon plan, construction, or ornament. Church building was a slow process, but before 1100 nearly all the English cathedrals and larger abbey churches had been knocked down and work had started on their successors. With the greater wealth of England to draw upon, the result was finer than anything in Normandy. Durham Cathedral, built 1096–1133, was the first to have a complete vaulted ceiling,

*See also *English Churches*, by R. R. Sellman.

and the massive piers of its nave still bear witness to the heavy-handed grandeur of the Norman earl-bishops.

Where the Saxons had preferred a square-ended chancel, the Normans introduced the rounded apse. In their larger churches there were three apses at the east end, or sometimes a passage behind the high altar from which radiated a 'crown' of apsidal chapels. The apse, which went back to the earliest Christian churches and beyond to the Roman town-hall basilica, left little room for the more elaborate ceremonial of the later Middle Ages, and most of them were in time pulled down to make way once more for larger and square-ended chancels.

The typical features of Norman churches are well-known—the heavy round pillars, semicircular arches, thick walls, narrow deeply-splayed windows, and squat square towers. The chevron or beak-head ornament of doorways, and the occasional wheel-windows at the west end, did something to relieve the general effect of massive gloom, but it is easy to see in these structures the spirit of the race that built them—proud and powerful, much concerned with strength and little with grace or beauty. The aspiring 'Gothic' to which they gave place a century later might have come from a different world, and certainly was inspired by a radically different outlook. Oddly enough, Norman work was sometimes less solid than it appeared. Pillars were often mere masonry shells filled with rubble; and where churches were built on a cross-shaped plan with a central tower resting on piers there was a tendency for this to collapse—as at Winchester in 1107 and Worcester in 1175. Norman architects had not reached the stage of calculating stresses and strains, and evolving devices to meet them; instead, they built heavily and hoped.

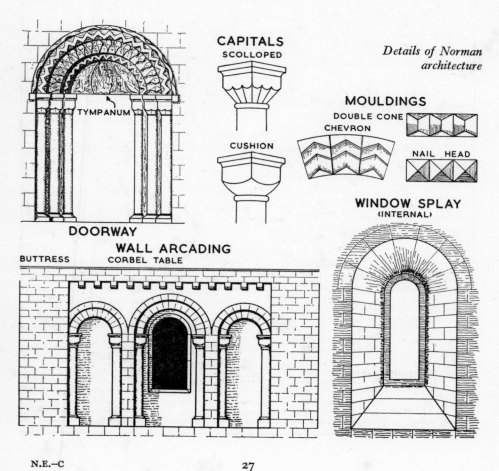

CAPITALS
SCOLLOPED

CUSHION

Details of Norman architecture

MOULDINGS

DOUBLE CONE

CHEVRON

NAIL HEAD

WINDOW SPLAY
(INTERNAL)

TYMPANUM

DOORWAY

WALL ARCADING

BUTTRESS   CORBEL TABLE

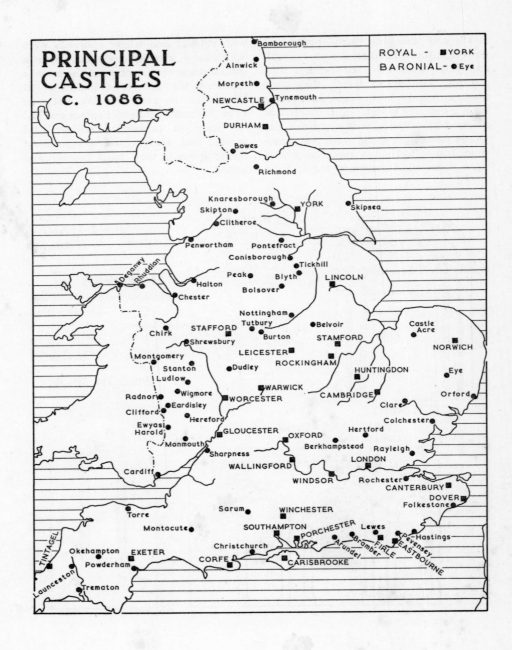

PRINCIPAL CASTLES C. 1086

ROYAL - ■ YORK
BARONIAL - ● Eye

Bamborough
Alnwick
Morpeth
NEWCASTLE Tynemouth
DURHAM
Bowes
Richmond
Knaresborough YORK Skipsea
Skipton
Clitheroe
Penwortham Pontefract
Conisborough Tickhill
Deganwy Peak Blyth LINCOLN
Rhuddlan Halton Bolsover
Chester
Nottingham Belvoir
Chirk STAFFORD Tutbury Castle Acre
Shrewsbury Burton STAMFORD NORWICH
Montgomery LEICESTER ROCKINGHAM
Stanton Dudley HUNTINGDON Eye
Ludlow Orford
Radnor Wigmore WORCESTER CAMBRIDGE
Eardisley Clare Colchester
Clifford Hereford
Ewyas Hertford
Harold GLOUCESTER OXFORD
Monmouth Berkhampstead Rayleigh
Sharpness LONDON
Cardiff WALLINGFORD Rochester CANTERBURY
WINDSOR DOVER
Torre Sarum WINCHESTER Folkestone
Montacute SOUTHAMPTON PORCHESTER Lewes
TINTAGEL Christchurch Bramber Pevensey Hastings
Okehampton EXETER Arundel FIRLE EASTBOURNE
Powderham CORFE CARISBROOKE
Launceston
Trematon

CASTLES*

One of William's first recorded acts on English soil, before the Battle of Hastings, was to build a castle at his temporary Hastings base: and the first concern of a Norman finding himself the new lord of a crowd of ugly-looking English rustics muttering in an unknown tongue was to do likewise. Castles had been unknown in Saxon times, but for a few erected on the Welsh Marches by Norman favourites of Edward the Confessor; and the English burh was different in purpose as well as design, being built and guarded by and for the people of the district in general. The king built castles to ensure his hold on the kingdom, against both attack from without and rebellion within. For this purpose William had one built in every county town, and at points of strategic importance such as the main ports and river-crossings. Garrisons were provided by knights doing their turn of 'castle guard', and also by a few men-at-arms and archers in regular pay.

*See also *Castles and Fortresses*, by R. R. Sellman.

The barons and many lesser landowners were concerned mainly to keep their own family secure and to have safe points from which to administer their scattered estates. William encouraged them to build castles for themselves, provided they recognised his right to garrison them himself in time of need.

Within a short time many hundreds of castles dotted the English landscape, all at first simple affairs of earthwork and timber to serve as stop-gaps until times were more settled and there was time and money to reconstruct in stone. The normal type in the early stages was the 'motte and bailey'—a mound surrounded by the ditch from which its soil was raised, crowned by a circular timber stockade, and an outer court of similar but less impressive earth- and timber-work. The main strength of the motte was in the steepness of the mound, since this made it practically impossible to destroy the stockade by battering or fire. Later on, when the mound had had time to settle, a 'shell-keep' of stone could be built in place of the timber, and the

A motte and bailey castle, reconstructed from remains at Brinklow, Warwickshire

bailey also walled with masonry, but many of the early mottes never reached this stage. After a generation or so the

HEDINGHAM CASTLE, ESSEX:

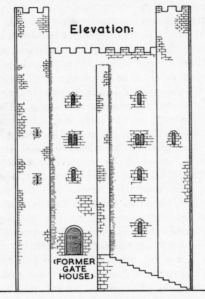

Elevation:

(FORMER GATE HOUSE)

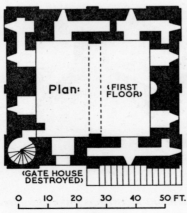

Plan: (FIRST FLOOR)

(GATE HOUSE DESTROYED)

0   10   20   30   40   50 FT.

lesser landowner often preferred the greater comfort and reasonable security of a moated house on the level. Living quarters on the motte must have been very cramped, and if they took the form of lean-to buildings against the rampart the arrangements would have been highly inconvenient for everyday life.

The great square keeps which we nowadays regard as typical Norman castles were in fact rare. They cost too much for the purses of all but the king and the greater barons, and they took a very long time to build. Nor could they be placed on an artificial mound, for the weight would be too much for foundations in made earth. Most of them were royal, and their gloomy harshness as living quarters mattered less when they had only to house a garrison. Some barons also built them, however, and housekeeping inside them must have been very trying for the ladies. In fact it soon became usual to live in the bailey, and to save the keep only for refuge in time of necessity.

The square keep shows the Norman mind with all its trust in deadweight and its lack of ingenuity. It was designed simply to keep an attacker out by mass of stone, and not to assist the defenders to beat him off. Walls up to fifteen feet in thickness, and ninety in height, with windows too small to squeeze through and a single door set high up and reached by a flight of steps and a drawbridge, effectually kept the enemy outside: but there was no means of shooting anyone at the base of the wall without leaning right over the battlements, and sorties were practically impossible. Hence sieges were mostly a question of which side

Doomsday Inquest

starved first.

For the purpose of holding down the English, however, the Norman castle was quite adequate. No rising by a collection of angry villeins had the least hope of success when it was denied the advantage of surprise and faced with the prospect of long inactive months of siege, and the king's castles inside the walls of towns kept an effective check on the possibly turbulent burgesses.

DOOMSDAY BOOK

When in 1086 William announced in the Great Council his intention of ordering a detailed survey of the kingdom, he showed the remarkable strength of the Anglo-Norman kingship. No other monarch in Western Europe for centuries attempted such a task, and none outside England had the authority and organisation to carry it through. His object was to find out, for tax purposes, what each estate was worth, but the information he asked for went far beyond this and has provided a mass of fact for historians. Sheriffs were ordered to assemble local juries of officials and villeins in each district, and the king's clerks, no doubt escorted by knights, questioned them on oath. The English were so impressed with the strictness of the enquiry that they likened it to the Day of Judgement, and 'Doomsday' it has been ever since.

The inquisitors were told to discover who held each manor in King Edward's time, and who now: how many hides it was rated at, and how many men and ploughlands were in the demesne: how many villeins, cottars, slaves, freemen and

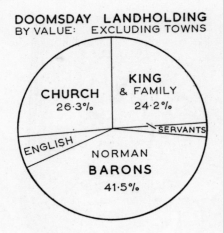

DOOMSDAY LANDHOLDING
BY VALUE: EXCLUDING TOWNS

KING & FAMILY 24.2%

CHURCH 26.3%

SERVANTS

ENGLISH

NORMAN BARONS 41.5%

sokemen the manor contained, and how much woodland and meadow: how many beasts, mills, and fishponds. They were to find out whether there had been any increase or decrease: what the whole, together, and the property of freemen or sokemen separately, had been worth before the Conquest, and what it was worth now. 'And the whole in triplicate' —before the Conquest, when William granted it, and at the time of the enquiry —'and if it could yield more'.

The English regarded this early version of the Income Tax form with mounting dismay, and in some parts there were riots or attempts at evasion by false returns. It was no use: the clerks

DOOMSDAY LANDHOLDING IN DORSET: 1086

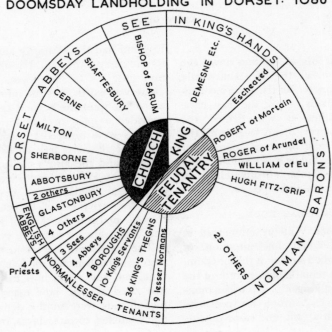

reappeared with the sheriff, the offenders were punished for perjury and the returns amended.

The Survey was not quite complete: it was not a census, and it did not cover most of the four northern counties. More unfortunate still, it omitted London, Winchester, Bristol, and some other boroughs. It was only concerned with property owners or heads of households, and so most of the clergy and women, and all children, were ignored. The actual number recorded is 283,242 out of a population estimated at about two million. Nevertheless, it tells us far more about early Norman England than we could possibly learn from any other source. We find some eight thousand Saxon landowners had been dispossessed, and only five hundred or so (including Lady Godiva) still held their diminished estates. Reckoned by value, the king and his family held a quarter of the country, the Church rather more, and over two-fifths was divided between Norman barons. Only a twentieth remained in English hands.

William's half-brother, Robert Earl of Mortain, is discovered holding 797 manors from Yorkshire to Cornwall; and his other half-brother Odo, Bishop of Bayeux, has 560. Indeed, Odo and three other Norman bishops between them hold more manors in England than belong to all the English bishoprics and archbishoprics! One very striking point emerging is the large number of English freeholders and sokemen in the districts of the ancient Danelaw, especially in Lincolnshire and East Anglia where there had been less excuse for confiscation: in Wessex there are hardly any. The Doomsday record shows how thoroughly and ruthlessly the Conquest had been exploited, and how dearly the English had paid for neglecting the art of war.

THE DEATH OF WILLIAM

In 1087, the year after the Doomsday inquest, William met his end after a fall from his horse while fighting in Normandy. Few grieved for him, for few had cause to love him, and his servants robbed his corpse and made off with the spoils. He was not 'great' in the sense that Alfred, or even Canute, had been: rather was he one who found a rare opportunity and knew how to make the most of it. Yet he had qualities which even the English unwillingly admired. Having once established his power, he generally kept the rules and respected law and custom even when he could have ridden roughshod over them. Conquest and subjection were bitter matters, but once they had happened men knew where they were with William. A less able Conqueror might have let loose an anarchy which would have been far worse.

William had had four sons; but the second, Richard, had already been killed in the New Forest. Between the rest, on his death-bed, he divided the inheritance. His eldest, Robert, who had helped his enemy the King of France against him, got Normandy and Maine: William Rufus, who had remained loyal, received the richer prize of England. For Henry, the youngest, there was no crown to spare, and he had to be content with five thousand pounds of silver from the hoard which his father had extracted from the English.

In an age when all history was written by churchmen, no ruler who hoped to leave a good reputation could afford to offend the Church. Rufus' repute has suffered ever since because of his light-hearted attitude to religion and his heavy-handed dealings with Church property. He was not as bad as the monks described him, and he had human and knightly qualities which contrast strongly with the cold grimness of his father. He could be generous and good-natured in his personal dealings; and while he crushed his enemies as effectively as the Conqueror had done, he was less ruthless in his methods.

At the outset his position was far from secure. The separation of Normandy from England was very awkward for barons who held estates in both countries, and some of them, led by Odo of Bayeux, rose in Robert's name in the hope of help from Normandy. Rufus promptly called out the fyrd, as well as the loyal Normans; an attempted invasion was beaten off at Pevensey, and Odo's castle at Rochester blockaded into surrender.

Like his father, Rufus made the most of his powers of raising revenue, feudal and otherwise. What aroused most indignation was his practice, after Lanfranc's death in 1089, of demanding enormous reliefs from new bishops and abbots or leaving an office unfilled for years while he enjoyed its revenues. This was inexcusable, though Rufus was by no means the only Norman king to do it. Canterbury itself was left vacant for four years, until Rufus fell seriously ill in 1093 and in fear of death hastily installed Anselm. Nevertheless he kept good order, which was the prime duty of a mediaeval king, and to him belongs the credit for recovering Cumberland and Westmorland from the Scots. The Conqueror had marched north in 1072 to punish continual Scottish encroachment, but Rufus did more. In 1092 he retook Cumbria and refounded and colonised Carlisle as a border fortress.

Neither Rufus nor Robert accepted the separation of England and Normandy as final; and in 1096, when Robert took the Cross for the first and greatest of the Crusades,* he was concerned both to raise money for his expenses and to guard against the conquest of Normandy by Rufus in his absence. He agreed with his brother for a loan of 10,000 marks (raised by a geld of four shillings on the hide) and that Rufus should administer Normandy as a pledge for the money while he was away. Robert served throughout the Crusade, surviving the capture of Jerusalem and the Battle of Ascalon, and won thereby far more credit than he had ever earned as a ruler. From England, however, there was little response. The only notable contribution came, significantly enough, from her seamen, who took a fleet of some thirty vessels into the Mediterranean, helped to capture Syrian ports and provision the armies, and joined in the attack on Jerusalem.

By 1100 Rufus was completely master of Maine and Normandy, and Robert was on his way home. Whether the latter could have found the money to redeem his duchy, or whether Rufus would have given it up if he had, was not put to the

*See *The Crusades*, by R. R. Sellman.

34

Rufus orders the rebuilding of Carlisle

test. Hunting in the New Forest that summer, Rufus was killed by an arrow shot by a certain Walter Tyrell. It might have been accident, or perhaps private vengeance, but there were circumstances which could have pointed suspicion at Henry. He also was hunting in the forest that day; Tyrell was one of his men, and after Henry seized the Crown Tyrell was richly rewarded.

HENRY I

It is not easy to understand at first sight why Henry left so much better a reputation than Rufus. Everything the clerics blamed Rufus for, Henry also did: ignoring his coronation promises, keeping sees vacant, taxing heavily, and quarrelling with Archbishop Anselm. His private life was by no means irreproachable —he left some twenty illegitimate children—and he was crueller in his revenges. But he reigned three times as long, and in thirty-five years he was to make advances of lasting importance in the royal authority and its means of government.

Rufus and Robert had previously agreed that whichever of them survived should have both parts of the Norman heritage, and on Rufus' death Henry had to act fast before Robert reached home from the Crusade. He at once rode to Winchester and seized the treasury, persuaded the doubters to declare him king, and had himself crowned. The events of 1066 almost repeated themselves, with Henry in the role of Harold. This time, however, the resulting invasion miscarried. When the forces of the two brothers met at Alton in Hampshire, neither felt confident enough to force a battle. Instead Robert recognised Henry's claim to England in return for a promise of £2,000 a year.

This only delayed a decision, and Henry made the better use of his time to prepare. By 1106 he felt strong enough for a final reckoning, and crossed to Normandy with an Anglo-Norman army. A single

35

one-hour battle at Tinchebray gave him the duchy, and condemned Robert to imprisonment for the remaining twenty-eight years of his life.

In Henry's time the feudal situation in England was clearly changing: there was no longer the same need for all Normans to hold together against the English, or for the king to rely on knight-service for campaigns and castle-guard. Fighting was mostly across the Channel, and for this purpose it was more convenient to raise a scutage and hire mercenaries. At the same time, the danger of baronial independence and rebellion was greater. It was thus essential to have the royal power directly felt all over the country, and to make government from the centre more effective. Henry therefore relied to a much greater extent upon ministers who were not barons but clerks promoted for loyalty and ability in his service, and these he sent round the country on circuit to assess taxes and do justice when sheriffs or barons defaulted. It was this which gained him the title 'Lion of Justice' and encouraged the English to regard him more as a national king and less as the head of a band of foreign usurpers. It seems Henry aimed deliberately at this result, since he married Edith, niece of Edgar the Atheling, at the beginning of his reign. It was certainly a political marriage, for after giving him one son (William, drowned in the White Ship in 1120) and a daughter (Matilda) Edith retired into a nunnery. It must have been clear to Henry that as the barons became less closely tied to the king he must rely increasingly upon the English.

In this reign we find for the first time a detailed account of the royal Household, and its increasing functions in government. It had three main divisions—the Chapel, the Hall, and the Chamber. The chief official of the Chapel was the Chancellor, whose daily salary and allowances amounted to five shillings, three loaves, two measures of wine, one candle, and forty candle-ends. Under him came the Master of the Clerks, the Chaplain, and the clerks and servants of the Chapel, all with proportionate payments. When the king travelled about the country his Chapel went with him— the men and the actual portable chapel, carried on packhorses. Wherever the king lodged a screen (cancella—hence 'chancery') was set up in the hall for the clerks to work behind, and there his writs and charters were made out and sealed. As head of this department the Chancellor was the most important official in the kingdom and the king's right-hand man.

The Hall was concerned with provisioning the Court, under the supervision of the Steward and the Master Butler. The Steward, with his staff of despensers of the Pantry and Larder, butchers, bakers, cooks, and servants, was responsible for food; the Butler, with despensers of the Cellar, cup-bearers and coopers, for drink.

The Chamber (bedroom) was also the safest place for valuables, and therefore we find the Treasurer as well as the Master Chamberlain as its head officers. The king's bed also travelled with him on packhorses, and the officials of the Chamber had to set it up and make it.

The Ewerer, who provided the king's baths at threepence a time, and the royal tailor, also belonged to this department.

Other important officials were the Constable, whose duty was to protect the Household and control the royal forces in war, and the Master Marshall. This latter was a sort of Court Quartermaster, whose subordinates went ahead to arrange lodgings as the court moved, and under him also came the royal huntsmen and archers and the 'hearthman' who received fourpence for making up the fire.

In Henry's reign these Household departments were developing fast into something like government offices, with a queer mixture of public business and personal service to the king's needs. By John's time it became necessary to separate some of these functions, and the Treasury and Exchequer no longer moved with the King but stayed at Westminster. The chief officials were far too important to make beds or hand wine, except perhaps on ceremonial occasions, and in time they were to become heads of government departments or titular officers with little to do except at Coronations. Most of them are still with us, and by some peculiarly English arrangement the Lord Chamberlain is now chiefly known as a censor of plays!

STEPHEN AND MATILDA

Both Rufus and Henry had had their claim to the Throne disputed, but with the support of the English and most of the barons both had made it good without much difficulty. When Henry died in 1135, however, the situation was different. He had left only one legitimate child, his daughter Matilda, and on three separate occasions he had compelled the Great Council to accept her as their future Queen. But the idea of a woman ruler was not popular, and neither was Matilda personally. From the age of eight she had lived in Germany, and had married the Emperor Henry V. After his death she became the wife of Count Geoffrey of Anjou, and she had spent little time in England. What people had seen of her did not attract: her pride, unpleasantness, and lack of tact had offended many. Henry's nephew Stephen was a very different character, frank, brave, and open-handed, and all his life had been spent either in Normandy or

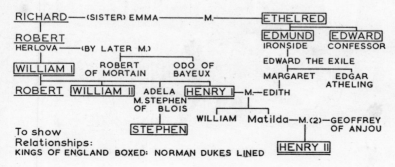

To show Relationships:
KINGS OF ENGLAND BOXED: NORMAN DUKES LINED

37

England. As soon as his uncle died, he repeated the exploit of 1100 and seized the Crown before his rival could appear. There was little objection, since Matilda had no following, and within three weeks he was crowned. To begin with all went well, and Matilda's complaints were ignored; but Stephen lacked his uncle's firm statesmanship. When he tried to enforce the royal authority in Henry's manner, the resentment which the barons had not dared express before broke forth into rebellion. At first Stephen dealt with it successfully, but amongst those he suspected of treachery was Bishop Roger of Salisbury, and his over-harsh treatment of this prelate and his relations offended the Church. The rebels naturally looked for a figurehead, and con- veniently remembered their earlier oaths to support Matilda. In fact they were fighting only for their own ends.

With this encouragement, the lady landed in 1139—to be immediately captured by Stephen. With more chivalry than common sense he released her, with a safe-conduct to join her supporters. Eleven years of war followed, in a con- fused and often desultory fashion, more marked by outrages on the countryside than by genuine fighting. Matilda's sup- porters never raised much of an army, and it was mostly a matter of attacks on castles which had to be starved out if they did not fall through treachery or surprise. The only notable engagement was at Lincoln in 1141, when Stephen was blockading the castle. The rebels

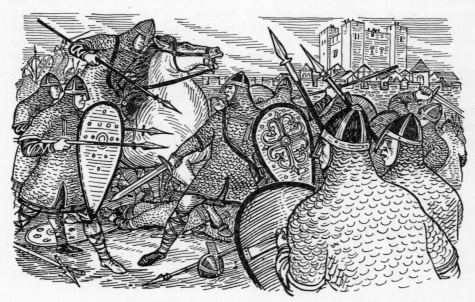

The capture of Stephen at Lincoln

arrived to relieve it, and the poor showing of Stephen's cavalry gave them an unexpected victory in which Stephen himself, fighting gamely, was taken. Matilda did not offer him a safe-conduct, but the capture of her own half-brother soon afterwards brought Stephen's freedom by exchange.

The next year we find Stephen besieging Matilda in Oxford castle, from which she escaped over the ice in the most picturesque episode of the war. After 1141 she never had much hope of victory, but neither could Stephen restore control over large areas of the country until she gave up and left for Normandy in 1148. The anarchy of this period was bad enough, but it has often been over drawn. A famous passage of the Anglo-Saxon Chronicle (still being kept up at Peterborough) describes a scene of unrelieved brigandage and disorder, but this cannot have applied to the whole country. Government continued in the areas Stephen controlled, and much of England was little affected. Stephen himself never lacked for money—he even sent some to Matilda's son Henry when the boy was in difficulties—and the royal estates and the machinery of tax-collection must have remained in working order in some areas at least.

In other circumstances Stephen might have been remembered as a good and popular king. It was his misfortune to come after seventy years of harsh and vigorous rule, and to reap the sort of trouble that descends on an easy-going schoolmaster who follows a strict disciplinarian. His lack of judgement at the outset let loose a situation which got beyond control, but he learnt from his errors and he never gave up. By his last years he managed to crush his enemies and restore something like order. He was an aging man by then, and tired. When young Henry crossed to England in 1153 and renewed the war. Stephen preferred to buy peace by acknowledging him as his heir. He had then in any case only a year to live.

The last, least, but personally most likeable of the Norman monarchs thus passed into history. His reign had proved at once the weakness and the strength of the Anglo-Norman monarchy: its dependence on the personal force and statesmanship of the monarch, and at the same time its ability to recover even after a period of anarchy when those qualities were once more forthcoming.

THE SCOTTISH BORDER

Though Rufus had for the time fixed the border with Scotland, it was by no means certain that his line would prove final. Ever since Lothian, with its largely English population, had been lost to the Scots in 1018, the border had ceased to correspond with any national division between Saxon and Celt. The Norman Conquest had driven more English across the frontier; and King David I (1124–1153) added an important Norman element as well by offering grants of land to induce barons and knights to settle. The Northumbrians, with their ancient tradition of independence and separatism, had as much in common with the Anglo-Scots of the Lowlands as with the Southern English, and it was quite possible that the border might eventually settle on the Tyne, the Tees, or even the Humber—or that the English

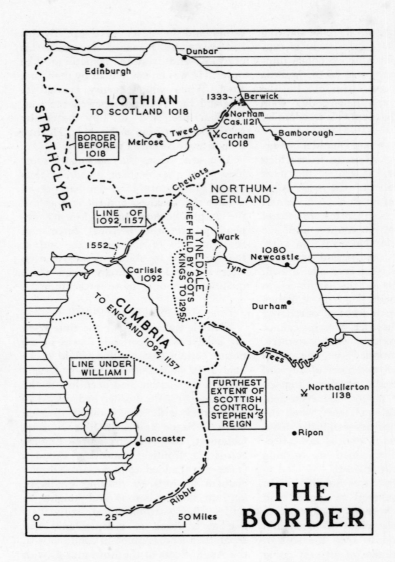

Dunbar

Edinburgh

LOTHIAN
TO SCOTLAND 1018

1333 — Berwick
Norham
Cas.1121

BORDER
BEFORE
1018

Melrose   Tweed   X Carham
1018

Bamborough

STRATHCLYDE

Cheviots   NORTHUM-
BERLAND

LINE OF
1092, 1157

TYNEDALE
(FIEF HELD BY SCOTS
KINGS TO 1295)

Wark

1552

Carlisle
1092

1080
Newcastle

Tyne

CUMBRIA
TO ENGLAND 1092, 1157

Durham

LINE UNDER
WILLIAM I

FURTHEST
EXTENT OF
SCOTTISH
CONTROL,
STEPHEN'S
REIGN

Tees

X Northallerton
1138

Lancaster

Ripon

THE
BORDER

Ribble

0 ———— 25 ———— 50 Miles

might recover Lothian.

It was largely a question of the respective strengths of the two kingdoms: and during the first three Norman reigns Scottish rulers were not strong enough to offer pitched battle, though they frequently raided into Northumberland in the time of William I and Rufus.

The Battle of the Standard

Stephen's reign, however, with England distracted by internal trouble, gave King David an opportunity of which he at once took advantage. In 1136 he retook Cumbria, and two years later he made a determined effort to conquer the Northern Shires. He invaded with a horde of Lowland levies and half-savage clansmen, led by mailed knights. Had he restrained the atrocious ravaging, killing, and slave-raiding of his uncouth followers he might have been more successful, but the very barbarity of the Scots drove the English to stand in their own defence when their king could do nothing.

Under the resolute earl-bishop of Durham the fyrd and feudal levy of Yorkshire mustered to bar the way at Northallerton. In the middle of their ranks towered the 'Standard' which gave the battle its name—the consecrated banners of the local saints Cuthbert of Durham, Wilfrid of Ripon, John of Beverley, and Peter of York, all hung from a ship's mast mounted on a cart.

As at Hastings, the English drew up in line and stood on the defensive, the knights dismounting to stiffen the fyrd, but their weapons had changed in the interval. There were many archers among them, and the rest carried long pikes or halberds in place of the shorter Saxon spear. There were far more Scots present, but their weakness in cavalry (and in

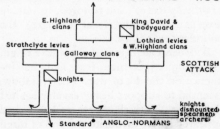

BATTLE of the STANDARD - 1138

41

discipline) prevented a repetition of the Hastings attack. David, who had doubtless drawn his own conclusions from Hastings, wanted the cavalry and archers to disorder the English ranks before the clansmen went in with claymores, but Highland pride insisted on going first. One body of Scots knights did indeed go right through the English line, but the gap was closed and all attacks on foot were beaten off. Disheartened as easily as roused, the clansmen refused David's final orders and straggled from the battlefield. He was compelled to follow, and the whole might of Scotland recoiled before that of Yorkshire.

The Anglo-Norman tactics in this Battle of the Standard, in which horses were left out of harm's way and all staked on a firm infantry defensive, foreshadow the very similar victories of the Hundred Years War in France. The bow, however, was not yet the murderous long-range weapon adopted from the South Welsh in the time of Edward I, and archers needed the protection of the pike. But though the victory at Northallerton was complete, Stephen was too weak to follow it up. With the ensuing disorder in England, David was able to advance his control to the banks of the Ribble and the Tees; and not till Henry II's time, in 1157, was Rufus' line restored, to remain (except for minor local changes) the boundary ever since.

Between Hastings and Stephen's reign, crusading experience had had its influence on the art of war. The crossbow, essential to support heavy cavalry against the light Turkish horse-archers, had appeared as the favourite weapon of hired troops on the Continent (though we do not yet hear of it in England) and the heavy infantry 'sergeant' was coming back into prominence. With an increasing use of scutage in place of knight-service, there was a demand for infantry: eight of them could be hired for the cost of a single knight with his train of servants and horses.

The Second Crusade came in 1147 while the 'troubles' were still not settled, but the English made their contribution— again by sea. An Anglo-Norman force left Dartmouth for the Mediterranean in a fleet reckoned at 164 vessels, and the same year helped the Portuguese to recover Lisbon from the Moors. One of these crusaders, Gilbert of Hastings, was chosen first bishop of the city.

THE MARCHER BARONS

The Norman Conquest was an event of outstanding and ominous importance for the Welsh as well as for the English. The two great earls of Chester and Shrewsbury, and the lesser Norman lords to the south, rapidly began minor 'Norman Conquests' of their own. William, Rufus, and Henry all led armies into Wales, but the movement was mostly one of semi-independent lords known as 'Marcher Barons', who ruled and exploited whatever they could conquer with little interference from the king. As in England, mailed cavalry made the conquest and castles held it. There was rapid progress in those parts of the country where horsemen could operate— along the North Coast, in Flint, Denbigh, and Montgomery, and right through the South to Pembroke. The Welsh, though generally worsted in battle, fought back

Wales and
the Marches

CONQUESTS OF
MARCHER BARONS

TEMPORARY CONQUESTS
IN BROKEN LINES.
ORIGINAL WELSH
KINGDOMS
UNDERLINED

0   10   20   30   40   50 Miles

with all the tenacity with which their forbears had resisted Vikings and Saxons; and repeated revolts such as that of 1094 did something to check the flood and retake its outposts. In the mountainous Principality of the North-West they maintained independence till the end of the thirteenth century; but in the South, in Pembroke, Gower, and parts of Glamorgan, whole districts were cleared of them in Henry's time to make way for

Flemish and English settlers who would have a common interest with the barons in defending the area. The Welsh bishoprics were at last brought into obedience to Canterbury, which they had refused for five hundred years, and Normans were installed in St. Davids and Llandaff.

The situation in the conquered parts was peculiar: they did not form part of the English kingdom (like the rest of Wales they were not formally incorporated till the time of Henry VIII) and their lords ruled almost independently apart from their personal allegiance to the King of England. Before long some of them intermarried with the Welsh and were on the way to absorption, while other lordships were inherited by barons whose chief estates and interests were in England. Marcher advance ceased by the end of the Norman period; and a Welsh national revival in the North, led by a succession of able and warlike princes, made the conquest of Gwynedd impossible till a king of Edward I's calibre should carry it through with all the resources of his kingdom.

THE MONASTIC REVIVAL

The first of the great monastic revivals to affect England in the Norman period was that of the Order of Cluny, then at the height of its renown on the Continent. It differed from previous Benedictine monasticism mainly in the organisation which held together all its member houses and in its concentration on continuous and splendid worship. In this it moved even further from Benedict's original insistence on manual labour—or indeed any kind of work outside the liturgy. Its corporate worship took so much time that there was hardly any left for study or teaching, and its part in public life outside the precinct was very limited. The ideal was continuous prayer and intercession on behalf of Christendom. The splendour and devotion of its services made a great impression on laymen who wished to endow a monastery to benefit from its prayer, and the first English foundation at Lewes c. 1079 was soon followed by others. The Order spread like a family tree from the mother house at Cluny, new foundations in turn sending parties of monks to start daughter houses. The abbot of each house had the right and duty of inspecting those which had 'hived off' from it, and the Abbot of Cluny, as far as practically possible, visited and controlled them all. Some three dozen Cluniac monasteries rose in England in Norman times, though a number of these were only small priories.

The Black Monks, within the Cluniac organisation or without, saw their greatest days in England under Henry I. In the long peace of his reign, with the upheaval of the Conquest over and their splendid new buildings finished, their monasteries were real centres of thought and learning. Secular schools, soon to develop into universities, had not yet arisen; and public business and the care of great estates had not yet diverted too much of the time of abbots and monks from the proper life of the community. It was also a great time of expansion for the Regular Canons, bodies of priests living by a Rule but in the world, serving a large church or running a school or hospital. St. Bartholomew's Hospital in London was founded by Rahere, Henry's minstrel, who became its first prior, and there were many such for lepers or for the ordinary sick.

But already on the Continent some were protesting against what they considered growing abuses eating into the proper purity and simplicity of monastic life. The increasing endowments of monasteries mostly took the form of manors, with the consequent growth of granges and the distractions of stewarding estates and controlling serfs. This, and the placing of many houses in towns, made

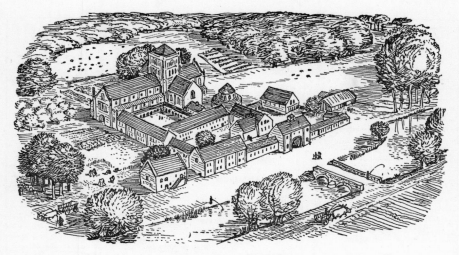

A Cistercian monastery

the original Benedictine idea of enclosed isolation impossible. Servants were everywhere, sometimes outnumbering the monks within the buildings, and the manual labour of the Rule had become a thing of the past. Magnificence of buildings and liturgy offended those who looked for primitive simplicity, and the requirement that all monks should be literate confined the monastic life to a narrow class. To meet these objections, and get back to the original spirit of Benedict's Rule, the Orders of Citeaux and of Savigny were founded at the turn of the century.

THE CISTERCIAN ORDER

The Order of Cîteaux had its humble origins in 1098, and that of Savigny fourteen years later. Their objects and methods were so similar that the Savigniac houses were merged in the Cistercians in 1147 and need not be considered separately. After a shaky start, Cîteaux rose to fame and became an established Order with the abbacy of Stephen Harding (an Englishman from Sherborne) and the arrival of St Bernard in 1112. Its spirit was puritan, rejecting alike the wealth, the ease of life, the art, and the elaborate worship of the existing houses. Dress, diet, and services were cut to the essentials of the original Rule, and all superfluous ornament of buildings and furnishings discarded. Time was thus found to restore the manual labour and the reading and private prayer of Benedict's day. The original monastic isolation from the world was also restored: monasteries were to be founded in remote districts, to break and work waste land for their own support, and not to accept endowments of manors and tithes. Servants were also excluded, all work

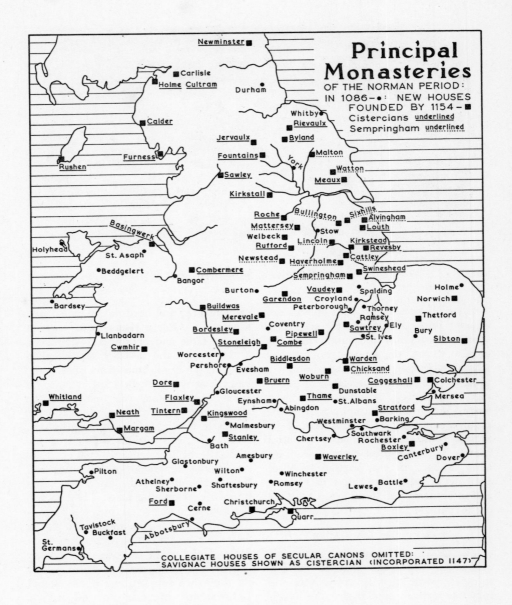

Principal Monasteries

OF THE NORMAN PERIOD:
IN 1086—●: NEW HOUSES
FOUNDED BY 1154—■
Cistercians *underlined*
Sempringham *underlined*

Newminster

Carlisle
Holme Cultram
Durham

Calder

Whitby
Rievaulx
Jervaulx
Byland
Fountains
Malton
York
Watton
Meaux
Sawley

Rushen
Furness

Kirkstall

Roche
Bullington
Sixhills
Mattersey
Alvingham
Basingwerk
Welbeck
Stow
Louth
Holyhead
Rufford
Lincoln
Kirkstead
Revesby
St. Asaph
Newstead
Haverholme
Cattley
Beddgelert
Swineshead
Bangor
Combermere
Sempringham

Bardsey
Burton
Garendon
Vaudey
Spalding
Holme
Croyland
Norwich
Peterborough
Thorney
Thetford
Buildwas
Ramsey
Llanbadarn
Merevale
Coventry
Ely
Bury
Bordesley
Pipewell
Sawtrey
Sibton
Cwmhir
Stoneleigh
Combe
St. Ives
Worcester
Biddlesdon
Warden
Pershore
Chicksand
Evesham
Woburn
Dore
Bruern
Coggeshall
Colchester
Whitland
Flaxley
Thame
Dunstable
Mersea
Eynsham
St. Albans
Neath
Tintern
Kingswood
Abingdon
Stratford
Margam
Malmesbury
Westminster
Barking
Stanley
Chertsey
Southwark
Rochester
Bath
Boxley
Amesbury
Canterbury
Dover
Glastonbury
Waverley
Pilton
Wilton
Winchester
Atheley
Shaftesbury
Romsey
Lewes
Battle
Sherborne
Ford
Cerne
Christchurch
Quarr
Tavistock
Buckfast
Abbotsbury
St. Germans

COLLEGIATE HOUSES OF SECULAR CANONS OMITTED:
SAVIGNAC HOUSES SHOWN AS CISTERCIAN (INCORPORATED 1147)

being done by the monks themselves or by 'lay Brothers' who were under monks' vows. These lay brothers were a remarkable development, opening the monastic life to the simple and illiterate who had been long excluded. They spent less time in church, and more in labour, than the full monks, but they were an integral part of the community.

Hitherto recruitment to monasteries had been mostly through 'infant oblation'—the admission of children at an early age to be trained in the house and to take their vows at adolescence. The Cistercians would take no-one under sixteen, and then insisted on the full year as a novice which was a long-neglected part of Benedict's Rule. They therefore kept no school, and at first they even forbade the writing of books.

To maintain standards and uniformity, the Order had a constitution and a system of control much stricter than that of Cluny. The method of inspection was similar, but in addition there was an annual assembly of all abbots in General Chapter at Cîteaux.

It was an easy matter to found a Cistercian monastery. All that was needed was the grant of waste land of no value, and the monks themselves would put up temporary wooden buildings to serve until they had time to replace them with stone. The Order therefore, at first, avoided the complications of the feudal system. It owed no knight-service, holding all land by frankalmoign, and had no manors to administer. Outlying areas were worked through granges staffed with a rotation of lay brothers, without taking the monks proper from the choir and the precinct.

The first Cistercian house in England was at Waverley in Surrey (1128) but it was in the North that they made their greatest impact. Here, in an area poor by nature and long neglected, cleared of monks by the Vikings and wasted by the Conqueror, they found exactly the kind of land they sought. Their first houses at Rievaulx and Fountains (1132) soon sent out parties to found others, and the Order spread with such rapidity that by the end of Stephen's reign there were more than fifty such monasteries (including those founded by the Savigniacs). Many of these were to play an outstanding part in the developing of the countryside, making the wastes habitable and productive and in particular introducing sheep-rearing to parts unsuitable for the plough. Such was the flood of recruits in the early days of enthusiasm that Rievaulx is said to have sheltered 140 monks and 500 lay brothers by 1167. In the long run this very success in attracting numbers was a cause of failure to maintain the original simplicity and seclusion; but up to the end of the Norman period the Cistercians were outstanding in an outstanding time of English monasteries.

The Cistercians' example had much influence outside their own ranks, and one peculiarly English result was the Order of Sempringham. Gilbert, rector of the Lincolnshire village of that name, was the confessor of a local community of nuns, and following Cistercian advice he added to it a body of lay sisters, and another of lay brothers to look after their estates. As the community grew beyond the scope of a single priest, he then added a small house of canons to serve its spiritual needs. With papal approval

Monks in cloisters, copying

(1147) this became the model for a group of double monasteries, mainly in Lincolnshire, known as the Gilbertines or Order of Sempringham. Before his death in 1189 there were about a dozen such houses, with some 1500 nuns and half as many canons, besides the lay members of both sexes. The buildings were designed as two completely self-contained communities on the same site, priests and nuns meeting only for the sacraments and worship. Though the Order covered a small and compact area compared with the great international ones, it had its central organisation under the Master of Sempringham and a General Chapter in which the nuns were fully represented.

THE MONASTIC LIFE

The Black Monks followed Cistercian example in giving up infant oblation, recruiting their members instead mainly from boys sent by their parents for training or from men of mature age who had been educated in the new schools outside the monasteries. They did not, however, reintroduce manual labour in fields and gardens, which remained the business of serfs or abbey servants. The Cistercian daily time-table found room for some four hours of this, but the original Benedictines preferred reading, writing, or their particular crafts of manuscript copying and illumination.

The day began about 2 a.m., when all left the dormitory (wearing their habits, in which they slept) for the night services of Mattins and Lauds, followed at dawn by Prime ('first hour'). After this they were free to read or work till about 8 a.m., when they washed and said the office of Terce ('third hour'). Directly afterwards all went to the Chapter House adjoining the church, where a chapter of the Rule was read, faults were confessed and punished, and business discussed. Another work period brought them to Sext ('sixth hour'), High Mass, and Nones ('ninth hour') after which in winter there was dinner about 2 p.m. In summer, when the day was longer, there were meals at midday and in the evening. After dinner came a period for reading, private prayer, or relaxation till Vespers about 5 p.m., after which there was a short break for a drink in the refectory, then Compline, and finally bed (in winter) about 6.30. On feast days, and especially in Cluniac houses, the services were much longer and the other periods correspondingly short.

As long as outside affairs were not allowed to interfere, it was a regular, disciplined, and austere life; and to the mediaeval mind the monks were not only engaged in saving their own souls but also through their prayer and worship helping laymen who could not give their full attention to religion. This is shown by the practise of 'confraternity', by which lay benefactors were enrolled on the community's lists, admitted when their end was near to the monastic habit and the infirmary, and after death buried and prayed for as if they had been monks. King John's interment at Worcester in a monk's gown was an example of this, and not a personal dodge to deceive St. Peter.

Monasteries also performed some practical service for the outside world, though the extent of this has often been exaggerated. Their teaching does not in fact seem to have catered for many besides those intending to become monks, though they sometimes endowed and supported schools outside their walls. Their hospitality to guests, pilgrims, and the poor was more marked at this time than in later centuries, and there are instances of jewels being stripped from the shrines and sold to find money to support floods of refugees in times of distress and disorder. It could be—and has been—argued that they took in tithes and endowments far more than they ever dispensed in charity, but this charge is truer of the later Middle Ages. Certainly the growing practice of presenting churches, with their tithes, to monasteries was to have unfortunate effects in the parishes; it meant that the priest was often a 'vicar' or deputy for the monastery, drawing only a fraction of what the village paid in tithe.

Probably the most striking fact about the monasteries of later Norman times is the immense proportion of the population inside them. We nowadays think of the monk as a rare and dedicated individual, so exceptional as to be capable of a standard of sanctity quite beyond the ordinary man. But by Stephen's reign it

is reckoned that one man in every fifty was a monk or canon. Even granted the greater piety of the period, it was too many; and even for their numbers their wealth was too great—something like a quarter of the total income of the country. The effects of this were not yet serious, but they were bound to show when the first enthusiasm cooled. Paradoxically, the weaknesses which caused so much criticism of monasteries in late mediaeval times and helped to justify their dissolution were a direct result of too much fervour by monks and lay founders and benefactors in the period of their greatness.

THE MANOR

The Norman Conquest had no noticeable effect on farming methods. Normandy was no more advanced in this respect, and the old Saxon agriculture survived unaltered. Over most of the country apart from the North and West the two- or three-field system continued, the former gradually giving way to allow two-thirds rather than a half of the arable fields to be cultivated at one time. For ploughing purposes these were divided into squarish blocks called 'furlongs', and subdivided into acre or half-acre strips under separate ownership. Ploughing began in the middle of each strip, the second furrow lying alongside the first but from the other direction, so that the sods were always turned inwards and the land ridged in a manner which can frequently be traced when ancient arable is now under grass. This helped drainage, and left a dip to mark the boundary of the strip. Ploughing might require as many as eight oxen, and had to be done by pooling beasts and labour, but sowing and reaping were each man's own business, as was the fixing of fences or scouring of ditches where his land adjoined the waste.

The land ploughed each year, whether a half or two-thirds, was sown partly in autumn and partly in spring, so that sowing and harvesting were spread as far as possible, and after harvest the fences were removed and the stubbles thrown open to the stock which had meanwhile lived on the waste or common. Meadow, as the only source of winter fodder, was very important. The animals were kept off it while the grass grew in early summer, and only allowed in when the hay had been made and carted. Though the meadow was in a sense 'common', it was usually partitioned with hurdles at mowing-time and lots drawn for the harvest on each plot.

This system required that all should do the same thing at the same time, and that they should help each other out when necessary. Not all land, however, even in open-field areas, came under it. Forest clearing was still going on, especially where population was growing, and ground so gained was generally enclosed and worked independently.

The great change which the Conquest brought was the fitting of English agriculture into the feudal system by dividing the country into 'manors' and making the great majority of farmers the tenants of

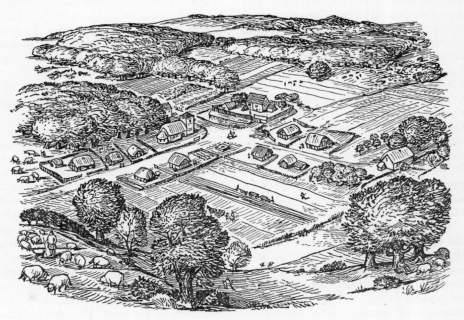

A Manorial village

a lord. In Southern England the manor was generally a feudally-organised single village, but this was not always so. In the Danelaw especially there might be two manors in one village, or more than one village in a manor. In theory the lord of the manor, like a king in miniature, was universal landlord, and all held of him in return for services. In fact this was never completely true. Doomsday lists about one in eight of the population (mostly in the Danelaw) as 'free tenants', who could defend their right to their land in the shire court, or sell it and go where they chose. The services they owed were often nominal, and never included weekly labour. Generally they helped at harvest time, and paid a small money rent, rather in recognition of the lord's authority than for their land. Oddly, a free man might be much poorer than a villein. Free land, unlike the rest, could be divided between several heirs, and the result might make a very poor holding. The Sokeman was also free, but his land was not. Because of the land, he was subject to the 'soke' or jurisdiction of the lord; and though he could leave the manor if he chose, he would forfeit his land if he did.

Free tenants were really relics of another age, who did not properly fit into the new system. By far the majority of countrymen were now unfree, though there were few actual slaves and these were soon absorbed into the lower ranks of the serf class. The classic test of unfreedom was liability to perform weekly service of a kind not laid down in advance: 'he knoweth not in the evening what he shall do in the morning'. It was a vital distinction, for the unfree were subject to the lord's court and could not get the protection of royal justice except in cases of 'life and limb'. Nor could the unfree easily get their freedom: officially they had no property and could not buy it, though there were ways of getting round this. The later loophole of winning freedom through successfully lasting out a year and a day in a chartered town was not yet open, and they could not enter the Church or a monastery without the lord's leave. All unfree men were tied to the manor, and if they left it they could be brought back and heavily punished. It might be hard to catch them, but it was harder still for a fugitive serf to find a living elsewhere.

On the unfree fell the full burden of the feudal super-structure, through their labour on the lord's demesne land and their liability to a mass of dues and taxes. They could be 'tallaged' whenever the lord needed money, charged for the use of the manor mill and oven, and mulcted of their 'best beast' as death-duty—a crushing matter for the heir if there were

A manor-house interior

only one ox or cow. They were fined for selling an animal, or allowing a daughter to marry, outside the manor (because both reduced the manorial 'stock') and they had to provide regular seasonal dues in kind such as the Christmas poultry and the eggs at Easter.

The heaviest burden was the weekly labour service, generally three days work for a full villein with a holding averaging thirty acres. This was not quite as bad as it sounds, for though the working day started at dawn it was often reckoned for this purpose to end at three in the afternoon, or even at midday. Nor did the villein have to do the work himself, if he had a grown son or could pay a hired man to take his place. People with only a few acres, known as cottars or bordars, owed proportionately less service, and made up their living by wage labour or by a craft such as smithing or working

the mill. At harvest, however, all must turn out in person, with their whole family, to get in the lord's crops before they dealt with their own.

The Manor Court, which all tenants must attend, took over the direction of agriculture from the old village moot and also most of the minor criminal business which had formerly gone to the court of the Hundred. It registered transfers of land, collected fines and dues, and settled disputes. For police purposes all unfree men over twelve years were enrolled in Tithing or Frankpledge groups, and made responsible for producing their accused members to justice or sharing the penalty. It was normally the sheriff's business to hold the 'View of Frankpledge' in the Hundred Court and collect the fines from those not enrolled; but many lords took over this duty themselves, with or without official approval, for the sake of the profits. Free men were exempt, because their land in a sense stood pledge for their good behaviour.

The results of the Norman Conquest were depressing, if not actually disastrous, for the great mass of English small-holder farmers. It did nothing to help their farming, but it provided an efficient system of extracting from them the profits of their labour. Before the Conquest there had already been many whom evil times had compelled to 'commend' their land to a lord, but they had still mostly been free men if no longer freeholders. For generations the process of degrading free men into villeins, and increasing the burden of service, continued. But though it was an oppressive system, it was on the whole an orderly one. If much of a man's work was on another's land, at least he had a fair chance of reaping what he had sowed on his own.

The Conquest was a set-back, but not a permanent turning-point, in the history of English towns. The immediate effects were, as everywhere, drastic: houses were knocked down wholesale to make room for royal castles, and the 'farm' or annual rent to the Crown was increased at a time when population had fallen. In some towns, like York, Shrewsbury, Norwich, and Southampton, French communities were settled, and for the time kept their own customs, court, and law of inheritance and left the English to pay all the taxes. Neighbourly feeling in such places must have been at a discount. The Doomsday record shows how much some towns suffered. At Lincoln 166 houses and at Shrewsbury 51, were destroyed for the castle, apart from many others derelict by 1086, and at Oxford the surprising number of 478 was written off as ruined or incapable of paying geld.

A cottage interior

53

Several places seem for a time to have lost half their population. Seaports which had traded busily with Scandinavia lost their livelihood when this connection was broken, and it was long before French and Flemish commerce developed sufficiently to take its place.

All the larger towns had grown up under the protection of the Saxon kings, and nearly all of them remained direct tenants of the Crown. A few exceptions, like Leicester, were granted to barons; but most baronial towns were new post-Conquest foundations, especially on the

PLACES NAMED IN BRACKETS WERE PROBABLY BOROUGHS

Boroughs under William I

A street scene

Welsh borders, where privileges were offered to anyone who would settle in the hope that trade (from which the baron could profit) would grow. Some such took root, but others never grew beyond the size of a village and either disappeared or were reduced to the status of a manor.

The burgess might feel hard-done-by, but he was less depressed on the whole than the countryman and had more hope of improving his position with time. He was personally free, and free also from the duty of attending the shire court, though unless his town were specially chartered he still had to submit to the sheriff's tax collection. Towns had a Portmoot of their own, and London also a weekly Husting or indoor court in the Guildhall. In the Guild Merchant the larger towns possessed an organisation which had a monopoly of business inside the borough and could raise money for public purposes, even before they acquired a mayor and corporation.

As always, Doomsday Book is our chief source of information for the period. It lists about eight thousand burgesses altogether, but this omits London and some other important places, as well as families and dependants. Estimates from its entries, admittedly uncertain, would give York a total population of about 8000, Lincoln and Norwich about 6000. These were the largest towns outside the capital, whose inhabitants at the time we might guess at 20,000 without being very far out. But most boroughs were very small. Some, in fact, hardly counted as towns at all, and were boroughs only because some king had favoured them with minor privileges. Even the larger towns were still partly agricultural, with arable and meadow outside the walls. Port Meadow at Oxford preserves to this day the memory of the farmer-burgesses of early times.

Doomsday details the dues and duties owed to the king, and shows that the towns made a well-defined contribution (dating from Saxon times) to the defence

55

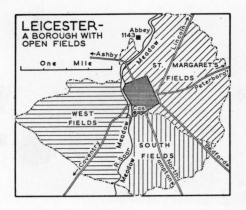

LEICESTER –
A BOROUGH WITH
OPEN FIELDS

of the realm. Dover supplied the king with twenty ships and crews for a fortnight, and even inland towns like Leicester and Warwick sent horses, men, or money towards the fleet. For land expeditions most towns found a fixed number of men, or a pound of silver in place of each if they paid in cash. Some, however, had more picturesque duties: Norwich provided hounds and a bear for baiting, with cash and honey, as well as money and a palfrey for the queen, and Shrewsbury found an armed escort when the king lodged there or hunted nearby.

The towns remained minting centres, as in Saxon times, and for a while the English moneyers (who were much better

craftsmen than the Normans) continued to turn out the best-designed and most reliable coinage in Western Europe. The silver penny was still the only English coin, and since at this time it represented the value of a day's unskilled labour there must have been a crying need for something smaller. It could be cut roughly into halves and quarters. It could also, unfortunately, be clipped round the edges (since it was thin and the metal soft) and taxes paid into the Exchequer were tested by weight. 240 pennies should have weighed a pound, but in practice they often fell short.

When Norman minters took over in Henry I's reign the standard fell, and in 1124 Henry summoned them all to Winchester for court-martial. Most were found wanting, and lost their right hands as well as their jobs. Each moneyer's name appeared on the back of his coins, so they were easy to trace: and in the Stephen-Matilda troubles some were faced by the problem of whose name should appear on the front. To strike coins with the name of Stephen, or Matilda, was a declaration of allegiance that might prove awkward if they, and the maker, fell into the hands of the other side. Some got round it by putting neither, and filling the space with the meaningless legend 'Pereric'. The number

Coin of William I

Coin of Henry I

56

of mints was gradually reduced during Norman times to about half, by eliminating the smaller places, but new ones were started in border towns like Pembroke, Newcastle, and Carlisle.

With Henry's reign some of the larger towns began to make progress. The famous fairs of St. Giles at Winchester, St. Ives, and St. Bartholomew (London) were founded by his grant, and both London and Lincoln attained considerable, if temporary, privileges. In 1130 Lincoln bought for 200 marks of silver and four of gold the right to keep out the sheriff and deal directly with the king as a tenant-in-chief, choosing its own Portreeve and collecting and paying the royal dues without outside interference. Two years later London, for a hundred marks, got the privilege of electing its own sheriff, who was also sheriff of Middlesex. Londoners were exempted from Murdrum (fines for slain strangers)

and geld, from trial by battle, and from tolls and customs at other ports, in return for a fixed annual payment or 'farm' of £300.

Such bargains were to become very common in later times whenever kings were in need of ready money, but the difficulty was to persuade the king or his successors to keep them once the cash was spent. Under Stephen London found herself back where she started, and she did not get the full liberties of a chartered corporation till the end of the century.

London, with its repaired Roman wall enclosing half a square mile, was already far ahead of any other town. Even before the Conquest there was a thriving trade with Denmark, Germany, Flanders, and Northern France. Its citizens had—and surprisingly kept—hunting rights in the Chiltern forest. Their numbers were enough for their militia to be something

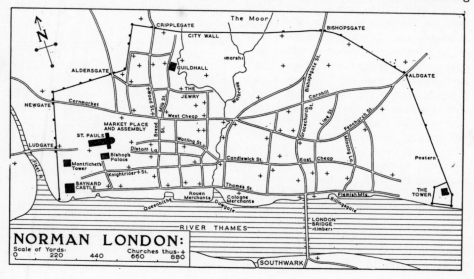

NORMAN LONDON:
Scale of Yards:
0   220   440   660   880   Churches thus +

57

of a power in the land, though they seldom used it outside the walls. Their refusal to accept Matilda in her brief time of success spoiled her one chance of the Crown, and in 1145 they mustered on Stephen's behalf and marched as far as Faringdon in Berkshire to capture a castle from Matilda's faction.

The city was large enough to be organised into 20 (later 24) wards, each with its wardmoot and alderman, and there were over a hundred churches. So many barons and monasteries wanted a foothold in the city that it was dotted with 'sokes'—private jurisdictions which were a headache to the authorities because they had no power to arrest the inhabitants unless they could catch them in the middle of the road. One of these belonged to the Scottish kings, who were also Earls of Huntingdon, and its site is still called Scotland Yard.

But even London, overawed by the royal Tower within its walls, never dared defy the Norman kings. In later times, as town wealth grew and kings were more pressed for money, charters which gave independence of the king's officials were to become general: but they never gave independence of the king. It was just as well, for in weakly-governed continental countries like Italy and Germany towns did emerge as independent republics, with lasting and evil effects upon the fortunes of those lands. The powerful monarchy which the Normans bequeathed was a blessing in the long run, if a somewhat disguised one at the time.

THE JEWS

One definite result of the Conquest, which particularly affected the towns, was the appearance of the Jews in England in the Norman wake. They were already established in the cities of Normandy, and many crossed almost at once to serve the conquerors as financiers and stewards of estates. Not being Christians, they were not affected by the Canon Law against taking interest on loans, but were barred from holding land. In Norman times they were allotted special districts in the towns, called Jewries, and allowed to practise their religion in peace. Like the forests, they were the special concern of the king, and the first three Norman rulers treated them reasonably and protected them and their goods against third parties. But against the king they had no protection, and from Stephen's time onwards they were taxed and pillaged mercilessly till they were ruined and expelled as no longer useful in 1290. Not all were concerned with money: some were distinguished doctors, and lectured on medicine and other sciences at Oxford.

TOWNS WITH JEWRIES IN THE NORMAN PERIOD

The Jews' House, Lincoln

The end of the Norman period saw a marked change in the attitude of people at large, as well as the king, towards them. Preachers of crusades stirred up mobs to attack them, foul rumours of murdering children for religious ceremonial were spread (exactly as they had been against early Christians) and the law forbade them to arm themselves against the massacres which followed. It was a shameful business, repeated at some time or other in every Christian country down to nineteenth century Russia and twentieth century Germany.

CONCLUSION

Some of the results of the Norman Conquest were obvious and immediate, while others matured slowly through the years. The first was the subjection of Englishmen, in the Church, the State, and the village, to an alien ruling class who cannot have numbered more than a hundredth of the population, and the concentration of the wealth produced by the many into the hands of this few. The daily life of the mass of men in town and country changed only in that, for the time at least, they were more tied and more taxed than ever before; but the effect on English civilisation, and particularly on the English language, was permanent. Anglo-Saxon ceased almost completely to be a language of scholars and literature. Latin became for most purposes the written, and Norman-French the spoken, tongue of the learned and the aristocracy. Few Normans outside the Church knew Latin, and most must have learned enough of the local English dialect to make themselves understood; but all continued to speak, and to teach their children, the tongue which was universal to their own class on both sides of the Channel. Even when their lower ranks began to intermarry with the English, as they did by late Norman times, the language and the social life of their households remained French for at least another century. For hundreds of years English was seldom written, and in that time it lost the elaborate declensions and inflections of Anglo-Saxon. In the long run this was all to the good, for its grammar became the simplest in the world; and when by the fourteenth century it once more emerged as the language of the Court and of literature it had also, by absorbing a mass of French and Latin words, acquired the richest vocabulary. Shakespeare could not have expressed himself in Anglo-Saxon; and without these developments English could not have become, as it is today, almost a universal tongue.

Before the Conquest the English monarchy, though powerful in strong hands like those of Canute, had shown distinct signs of decay under Edward the Confessor. There was a plain danger that it might relapse like that of France into a titular headship, with real power exercised by local Earls. From this the Norman kings saved England. By grafting their own brand of strictly controlled feudalism upon English methods of government, by their personal forcefulness and efficiency (apart from Stephen) and by introducing the beginnings of a civil service, they established the English monarchy in a fashion which allowed it to survive later episodes of baronial revolt and weak kingship and to remain throughout the Middle Ages the strongest in Europe. This was of enormous benefit in an age when the need was for order, and when freedom meant only the liberty of the strong and unscrupulous to oppress the weak.

Apart from this, the most outstanding effect in the long run upon English history was that the country was drawn out of its isolation and linked with the lands of ancient civilisation and new revival in the South. Without the Conquest it is probable that the English would long have remained a semi-Scandinavian people, looking for their main contacts to their kindred across the North Sea, and little influenced by the great developments of culture and the spirit which swept the continental lands. This was not an unmixed blessing—it involved English resources in long and futile wars over the French claims and possessions of English kings—but the benefits far exceeded the disadvantages. England became much more an integral part of Western Christendom than she had been in Saxon times, or than the Scandinavian kingdoms remained throughout the Middle Ages.

To the English at the time the Conquest

must have seemed, and largely was, an unmitigated disaster. Subjection to disdainful and overbearing foreigners could not be a light matter to men with the proud traditions of Alfred. Nor could the Normans be easily absorbed into English society, as the Danes with their similarity of language and background had been. In time absorption was bound to come; but by then England herself had changed. The Saxon past was too deeply rooted to be brushed aside with the Saxon nobility, but the England of pre-Conquest days could never return. For good or ill, and in the long run mostly for good, the ancient heritage was influenced by Norman practical ability and enriched by the reinvigorated spirit of the Mediterranean lands. The descendants of Harold's thegns and of William's knights were both the gainers.

aid: a feudal payment to an overlord to meet special expenses, confined by Magna Carta to three purposes— knighting of the lord's eldest son, marriage of the lord's eldest daughter, and ransoming the lord from captivity (e.g. Richard I).

Anselm: 1033–1109: Italian; eventually entered monastery of Bec in Normandy during Lanfranc's priorate: took monastic vows 1060, prior 1063: achieved a great reputation for learning and sanctity. Several times visited England while Lanfranc was Archbishop, and generally regarded as the man to succeed him. Consecrated to Canterbury 1093, but soon at loggerheads with Rufus: left England to appeal to Pope 1097, and did not return till after Rufus' death. Recalled by Henry I, but denied the king's claim to install him and require homage: again in voluntary exile 1103–6, after which he came to terms with Henry and died in office. Later canonised.

Atheling: Saxon term roughly equivalent to 'prince'.

baron: term originally meaning simply 'man', and hence in early Norman times those who held land direct of the king and were his 'men' in a special sense. Later applied only to the more important tenants in chief, but still used in its original sense of the men of the Cinque Ports who stood in special relationship to the Crown.

Bayeux Tapestry: Strip of embroidery 231 feet long by 20 inches wide, made to the order of Bishop Odo of Bayeux for the adornment of his new cathedral, and probably designed and made at Canterbury soon after the Conquest. Takes the form of a 'strip cartoon', illustrating events before and during the Norman Invasion.

Benedict (St.), Rule of: detailed regulations for the monastic life devised by St. Benedict for his monks at Monte Cassino in Italy in the early sixth century, and subsequently the basis of mediaeval monasticism. The Rule includes the triple vow of poverty, chastity, and obedience, and legislates for an enclosed community life of worship, prayer, and manual labour.

Cinque Ports: group of Kent and Sussex ports, originally the 'Five' after which they are named (Hastings, Romney, Hythe, Dover, Sandwich) with Rye and Winchelsea added later. Many smaller places were attached to one or other of these ports to help in carrying out the obligation to provide the king with sea transport and fighting ships (which dates at least from the Confessor). Throughout most of the Middle Ages the main naval standby of English kings, and enjoying in return unusual privileges.

danegeld: originally a war-time tax raised to buy off Danish invaders, and afterwards maintained as a convenient form of direct tax on land throughout Norman times. Assessed on the hide (which see), generally at the rate of 2s. but sometimes twice or thrice this figure.

Danelaw: approximately the area north and east of the line London-Chester, conquered by the Vikings in the later ninth century, where Danish law or custom survived into Norman times. In this area the Hundreds were called 'Wapentakes'.

excommunication: solemn exclusion of an individual from the sacraments and services of the Church, involving damnation if he died unreconciled, and including a similar threat against anyone who associated with or helped him.

fair: annual gathering of merchants from a wide area for trade, sometimes of international importance, and generally lasting a fortnight; distinct from the weekly one-day market for local business.

Godwine: 990–1053: made Earl of Wessex by Canute in 1020, and remained throughout his life the most powerful man in England next to the king.

Harold: 1021–1066: second son of Godwine, made Earl of East Anglia in 1045; Godwine's heir after the death of his elder brother Sweyn in 1051, and hence succeeded to his father's position and power in 1053. Travelled to Rome; twice defeated the Welsh; left only illegitimate sons.

Hereward: early life unknown: a tenant of Peterborough Abbey, on the appointment of a Norman abbot in 1070 he raised the tenantry in rebellion and fortified himself in the Isle of Ely where several outlawed English notables joined him. Escaped when the islands was captured by William in 1071, and continued for some time as an outlaw. According to some accounts killed in 1073, but by others eventually reconciled to William and long survived.

hide: Saxon unit of cultivated land, usually corresponding to a 'ploughland' of 120 acres, divided into 'virgates' of 30. As a taxing unit the Domesday hide varied greatly, from over 120 acres to as little as 40, apparently as a result of a rough assessment of the value of the land or through William allowing some estates to bear less than their share of tax.

homage (and fealty): ceremony by which every free tenant became the 'man' (homo) of the lord who granted him a fief or estate, followed by the oath of fealty or loyalty. Homage was 'done', and fealty 'sworn'.

housecarles: originally a bodyguard of more than 3000 men retained by Canute when he disbanded his Danish army in 1018, maintained and paid as part of the royal household. In later times mainly English, and often established on estates as thegns.

Hundred: ancient division of the shire, of uncertain origin and very various area, with a monthly court for the local freeholders: loses most of its importance with the growth of manorial courts in Norman times.

Lanfranc: 1005–89: born in Pavia (North Italy): studied in Italy and France, taught at the cathedral school of Avranches (Normandy): entered Abbey of Bec 1042, and shortly prior. Abbot of William's new monastery at Caen 1063. (for later events see text)

Marches: Saxon for 'borders' (compare German 'Mark') and hence the Welsh and Scottish borderlands. Adjective 'marcher'.

mark: weight of eight ounces Troy, and hence in money terms two-thirds of a pound of silver or 13/4: sometimes reckoned in gold, at nine times the value of silver.

thegn: originally one ennobled by a Saxon king for service as a personal retainer, but in later Saxon times the land-owning nobles and gentry with special war-service obligations and often local authority.

tithes: payment of one-tenth of produce or profits, originally voluntary and for the poor as well as the clergy. By late Saxon times compulsory, and used entirely for the support of the Church. The 'great tithe' of corn, beans, and hay went to the 'rector' or owner of the advowson (often a monastery) and only the 'lesser tithe' of other produce to the parish priest.

William I: 1027–1087: illegitimate son of Duke Robert of Normandy: became Duke 1035, but unable to establish his authority till 1047. Twice defeated French invasions, and enlarged his dominions by adding Maine and parts of Anjou. Married Matilda of Flanders. (for events after 1066 see text)

Witan: literally 'wise men': in Saxon times the body of advisers whom the king consulted on important business, including the ealdormen of the shires, the bishops, and the leading Household officials.

A SELECT BOOK LIST

By Elizabeth N. Bewick, A.L.A.

ALLEN, A. B. *Norman England.* ("New Project" series.) Rockliff, 1953. Illus. A project book for younger children, covering the social and political history, everyday life and costume, literature and learning of the Norman period in England.

BARLOW, F. *The Feudal Kingdom of England.* (History of England, Vol. 2.) Longmans, 1954. Maps, booklist. A history of the political, constitutional, economic, social, religious, military and cultural history of the period 1042–1216. Advanced.

DAVIS, H. W. C. *England under the Normans and Angevins.* Methuen, 13th edn. repr. 1957. A study of the social, political and economic history of the period. Advanced.

HARRISON, M. and WELLS, A. A. M. *Picture source book for social history: from the Conquest to the Wars of the Roses.* Allen & Unwin, 1958. Illus. An anthology from contemporary sources, illustrating the social history of the Middle Ages, including the Norman period.

KNOWLES, D. *The monastic order in England.* C.U.P., 1940. A history of its development from the time of St. Dunstan to the Fourth Lateran Council, 943–1216. Advanced.

MACLAGEN, E. *The Bayeux tapestry.* ("King Penguin" series.) Penguin Books, rev. edn., 1945. Scenes from the Bayeux tapestry, representing the Norman Conquest of England, with an introductory study of the tapestry, its history and contents.

POOLE, A. L. *From Domesday Book to Magna Carta,* 1087–1216. (Oxford History of England, Vol. 3.) O.U.P., 2nd edn., 1955. Booklist. The standard political history of the period for the older reader.

PRICE, M. R. *A portrait of Britain in the Middle Ages,* 1066–1485. ("Oxford Introduction to British History" series.) O.U.P., 1951. Illus. Social and economic history of the Middle Ages, including the Norman period.

QUENNELL, M. and C. H. B. *Everyday life in Anglo-Saxon, Viking and Norman times.* Batsford, 4th edn., 1955. Illus. Covers the period from the social aspect, the people and how they lived, their character, dress, houses, education and literature; with a chronological time-chart of events.

STENTON, (LADY) D. M. *English society in the early Middle Ages,* 1066–1307. ("Pelican History of England.") Penguin Books, 1951. Booklist. A study of early medieval society including the king's household and government, barons and knights, country and town, Church and people.

STENTON, SIR F. M. *The first century of English feudalism.* O.U.P., repr. 1950. A study of the feudal system in Norman England, its structure organisation and effect. Advanced.

STUART, D. M. *The story of William the Conqueror.* ("Story Biographies.") Methuen, repr. 1958. Illus. The life of William of Normandy and his conquest of England told against a background of the history of the period.

English historical documents: 1042–1189; edited by D. C. Douglas and G. W. Greenaway. Eyre and Spottiswoode, 1953. Illus. Select documents and narratives from contemporary sources relating to the history of the period, its government and administration, Church and people.

Norman England. B.B.C., 1959. Illus. booklist. Originally published in connection with a series of broadcasts, this brief but informative pamphlet covers all aspects of the Norman period, with many illustrations. It would be most useful as an outline for project work.

INDEX